WINNING

at the Stock Market

(while keeping your DAY JOB)

Ali Dada

Shield Crest

ISBN: 978-1-913839-20-8

MMXXI

A CIP catalogue record for this
is available from the British Library

Published by
ShieldCrest Publishing Ltd.,
Aylesbury, Buckinghamshire,
HP18 0TF England
Tel: +44 (0) 333 8000 890
www.shieldcrest.co.uk

To my Mother and Father who backed a twenty-three-year-old with an idea

To my Wife who has always supported me in everything

To my Children – you were my real target audience when I wrote this book

Contents

The Author

Ali Dada is a Chartered Accountant who specialises in Internal Audit, Risk Management and Business Transformation. He has been a speaker in a number of global conferences and has written a number of articles on subjects that range from Internal Audit, Stock Market and Commercial Aviation.

The Stock Market has been a passion, something he has pursued actively and increasingly since 1999, initially from being just a hobby to a point where it became a successful avenue of generating income.

This is Ali's first book which he felt compelled to write as a reference document for all part time investors to provide them with what he considers is a safe but profitable method to succeed in the stock market.

Ali is married with three children and currently divides his time between his home in the UK and his work in the Middle East.

Preface

Why do I invest in the stock market? It's because it gives me an unmatched sensation of victory. And that victory was achieved only because I came up with an original and unique idea that made it possible. It was my decision to enter the stock market; it was I who analysed the information that was available to everyone, and it was I who decided to do something with it.

Everyone else had the same opportunity, as the information is publicly available, but most either ignored it, analysed it incorrectly or weren't even aware of it. And whenever I complete a trade profitably as an individual investor, I beat a market where many others (some with much more time, information, skill and resources than I have) lost out. That is why I am in the stock market. Because I like to feel that joy of winning against the odds again and again. I like being the underdog that keeps winning.

It's not that I do not enjoy making the money that comes with such 'victorious' trades. After all, that is the primary and tangible reason for being in this business in the first place. But more than anything else, I enjoy spotting an opportunity and then creating a success out of it. Don't get me wrong, as I realise I may have come across as a crazed gambler, but what I do is anything but gambling, nor do I rely on sheer luck. Every transaction is based on analysis, reason and a lot of patience. There is, of course, an element of calculated risk in each transaction, but then isn't that the case for everything we do in life? The idea is to base an investment on a logical business case and within an acceptable level of risk.

The way I see it, the stock market presents an opportunity to everyone to make money and is available to anyone who has the awareness to recognise the opportunity and then analyse it enough. At the same time, if you jump in relying on pure luck, it can (and most probably will) wipe you out very, very quickly. It represents a fair opportunity as there is an equal risk for everyone who chooses to enter. It's all about how you make it work to your advantage.

Imagine this scenario, and it is a real one from one of my favourite trades:

08.00 on 28 October 2019

Imperial Brands (IMB), one of the largest tobacco companies globally, sees its share price drop again, and it is nearing its all-time low. The company has a brilliant financial record and dividend history. However, there are two challenges to bear in mind: the CEO has just left the company suddenly, and it is facing a legal challenge to its Vaping business in the US. It is also due to pay an announced interim dividend of 72p a share on 21 November 2019 and again on 20 February 2020.

<u>*Decision:*</u> *Buy at £18.15 a share.*

<u>*Rationale:*</u> *I do not believe the tobacco business will slump quite that easily and disappear, and the reaction is more due to the CEO leaving. If it does not rise, I can hold the share long-term due to its high dividend yield. My plan is to sell if the price goes up by 5% over my buying price.*

08.00 on 15 November 2019
IMB continues to drop for the same reasons explained above. My holding value is negative. *Decision: Buy more shares at £17.30 a share to increase holding and lower breakeven price.* *Rationale: I do not see any news in the market that would suggest the company is getting weaker. And the dividend is due next week. If I buy more now, I get an even better dividend yield.*
15.00 – 03 January 2020
Brokers begin upgrading IMB target price, and the news of a new CEO being appointed start to float. The share prices start to rise. *Decision: Sell at £18.95.* *Profit: £1.42 per share plus £0.72 per share dividend. That is a gain of 12.2%.*

My idea, my research, my move, my win! And there is a substantial profit as well to make it worthwhile.

That is precisely why I am in the stock market and why I have persisted with it. This is also what I want to inspire you to feel. I want you to use this book and tactics I have spelt out, so you know how to start, what to look for when selecting an investment opportunity, and develop your own investment idea that beats the market that you were not supposed to be successful in.

In its current form, the stock market is almost designed mainly for the large institutions and investment funds to succeed, as they have the financial might to be able to define how things flow. This book is to inspire and guide that underdog who dares to go out there and win against the odds!

Welcome to the stock market.

Introduction

"Every time you make money on a trade, you have beaten the giants of the stock market. And if you can do it again and again, you are not gambling. You have simply worked out a way of beating the odds that are stacked against you."

I am an individual investor and only trade using personal funds. I have never used any investment advisor or any fund. When any wealth manager approaches me with an offer to help me manage my funds, I ask them if they can exceed my 30% return on investment. If I let anyone else manage this for me, it will not feel like my victory. I have a day job too, so I do not dedicate all my time to the stock market. Nor do I have access to data, research or analysis a professional fund manager would have. I work with information that is available to all online. But over time, I have built up tactics and strategies that have helped me navigate the stock market profitably and with relative safety.

I decided to write this book to consolidate all that I have learnt since I began my trading life in 1999 as a twenty-three-year-old who had recently come across that fabulous Academy Award-winning movie *Wall Street*. Not that I wanted to indulge in insider trading like Gordon Gecko, but the idea of using a market to your advantage just sounded fascinating. I wanted to capture and explain all the tactics I tried, and all those ideas that worked well, and even things that did not work out well in this one document. Through this book, I have lived my entire journey once again.

One thing is a constant across all I have ever tried; the ideas have always been simple, easy to analyse and research, and eventually easy to execute. Simple things, in my experience, work surprisingly well.

This book is not for a person looking to become an instant millionaire on the stock market. I am sure it is possible, but I do not know how to do it. And whenever I tried something exceptionally ambitious, it did not really work that well for me. Therefore, I keep my approach simple and within practical limitations so that I can manage on a part-time basis, and I use data I can understand, analyse and keep up to date with.

I do not recommend a complex approach to a part-time investor, particularly to anyone starting out. Keep it simple and learn safely, and then when you have a history of a few successful trades, you will naturally evolve and develop your own tactics with experience.

This book is also not for someone who is a professional investor or trader—they have far more time, knowledge and access to information than an average person may have. I certainly do not claim to have such knowledge, but I have learnt to operate within my limitations that typically apply to the average non-professional, part-time investors with the time we can make available for this.

I wrote this book for a person who wants to try their hand at the stock market but does not have the time or inclination to research in detail, does not fully understand where to start, and wants to avoid the typical pitfalls that lead to loss. It is for a person who already has a day job but wants to do something else to make money with relative safety.

It is a book to help you start off slowly and profitably and then build a second, sustainable source of income that grows with time. You can always go to a fund manager who may be able to promise you a decent return on your investment. But if you want to feel the buzz of beating the market all by yourself and making money, then this book is for you.

One of the other objectives I also set for myself in writing this book was to try to explain what I believe is a relatively safe, simple and effective investment model that I have developed over time which has worked quite well for me. It took me the best part of two decades to eventually settle on it. I have stood by it since 2018.

The stock market can be a dangerous place for new entrants, particularly the target audience I am writing this book for. It offers an irresistible lure of massive gains, but more often than not, things don't quite work out if you jump in without knowledge. There are far too many cases of people going in to make a huge gain only to lose out all they invested. I do not want that to happen to you. Start off with a safe model, understand how it works, and then eventually decide how you want to change your baseline.

I did not have very good advisors. However, I did have a lot of common sense, restraint and a bit of luck, which kept me relatively safe. I did take some bad blows, but I learnt from them. I am trying to pass that on to keep you safe and successful.

I do not intend for this book to be a technical masterpiece full of jargon and buzzwords; I like to keep things simple and, more often than not, simple works best. I will answer all questions that I have been asked many times from people, from how to get started to how to select shares to invest in and when to buy, hold or sell. I will cover things that have worked for me and explain how they have worked well for me.

While this book largely reflects my experience of trading initially in Pakistan and then mostly in the UK, the approach in its entirety is largely transferrable to any stock market near where you are based or which you choose to invest in. Do not let the FTSE examples put you off by thinking that this is a UK specific book. I prefer to limit myself to the UK to allow myself to focus on a specific number of companies (a tactic that I recommend and have explained later in this book). But rest assured, this will apply to all stock markets.

Since I began, I have tried a few different approaches, and I had to adapt them every now and then. If I were to summarise my investment lifecycle in phases, here is the best way I can explain it:

Karachi Stock Exchange	
1998 to 1999	***Research*** I began by selecting around 16 KSE-100 companies and trend analysing them for six months daily on a manual spreadsheet. I relied on the daily opening and closing reports from a newspaper. Therefore, before I properly started, I had a fair idea of each share's high and low price trends. I would stick to these 16 companies till 2001 and focus only on them.
1999 to 2001	***First Trading Account*** My mother showed quite a bit of faith in me and let me use PKR 100,000 of her funds, and I opened a trading account with a neighbourhood broker. The market required all purchases to be settled by Friday, even if shares were purchased throughout the week. Trading was done on a phone call, so I had to buy my first ever mobile phone as an online trading option had not been introduced at the time. The day traders would buy throughout the week, hoping the share price would go up before they had to settle, and they could scoop out net gain. When those day traders (or gamblers as I like to think of them) would desperately sell on Friday (as most were unable to settle and were now trying to reduce their 'gambling' losses), I would buy with the money in my account and settle immediately. The share price would (more often than not) rise on a Monday when the traders/gamblers stepped in again, hoping to recover last week's losses. My first trade was Pakistan State Oil. I recall I made PKR 8,000 when I sold.

Karachi Stock Exchange (Continued)	
1999 to 2001	I had doubled my funds in one year. Such was my success that my broker thought I had inside information, while all I was doing was waiting for the gamblers to fold on Friday. If I could find a price that was low enough in line with my analysis for the 16 shares on my shortlist, I would buy. My mother then allowed me to add PKR 200,000 to my fund. And then I made my first mistake. I bought shares on an 'expert's' advice, and a few months later, 80% of my gains were gone. Around that time, I had to liquidate all my shares, as I moved from Pakistan to Saudi Arabia due to my career. I would never, ever invest on an investment tip from an expert again. I would be the only expert that I would rely on.
2002 to 2004	***Online Trading*** Once I moved to Saudi Arabia, I had a bit of money of my own. So I restarted trading through online trading options that were now available for Pakistan. Simple trend analysis was no longer successful, and the market had matured. Settlements were now on purchase and not on Friday. I did not realise a need to change my approach and did not make the additional effort to understand the market. This phase was easily the least successful investment phase in my life. Nothing really to brag about here. I sold out, prepared for a career move to the UK and decided to walk away...

London Stock Exchange	
2008 to 2012	***Return to the Markets*** ... until the bug bit back. Once I had settled down into my new life in the UK, and the stock markets began to go a little volatile due to the 2008 recession, I felt an old urge to get back on the horse. The financial data was more readily available, and I could pick a selection of companies and trends quite easily without having to prepare them myself. The strategy I opted for was to identify companies that were at or close to all-time low prices but with limited regard to their financial potential. I started conservatively and won far more often than I lost. Of the 25 trades I made, I profited in 20, along with some dividend. But the five I lost money in hurt quite badly, including one company that shut down on me. I learnt that junk shares were called junk for a reason.
2013 to 2017	***A Shift in Approach*** As I began to increase my funds in play, I began to redefine my strategy. Junk shares were out, and my focus shifted to stocks in companies that were constituents of either FTSE-100 or FTSE-250. Financial analysis became the basis for a decision. I defined my list of 25 companies that I would focus on and to which I would limit myself. I picked sectors that I would invest in and cut the rest out. This was the highest yielding phase of my investment career thus far, where my return on investment tracked at well over 30% per annum through a combination of trades and dividend. This phase resulted in a partial exit from the markets as it had allowed me to scale up my gains to a level where I could invest in property. I completed 49 trades in this phase, of which 45 made profits. The four trades I lost money in did hurt, but it was because I broke two rules: 1) I invested funds with a time limit, and 2) I did not cut my losses when I had the chance earlier.

London Stock Exchange (Continued)	
2018 to date	***A More Sustainable Long-Term Approach*** After completing my property trades, I began moving funds again into shares, but my appetite for aggressive and frequent trades had waned. I wanted to develop a more sustainable approach that yielded profits without worrying about the constant need to buy and sell. I wanted an approach that I could manage with my career and travel schedule, which was getting busier. The 2013 to 2017 phase required me to be awake and aware of when the FTSE opened while travelling extensively across the world for work. I missed out on closing a profitable trade in the middle of a night in the US as impacted by lack of sleep and severe jetlag, I locked my account out groggily, forgetting my trading password! Took a few days to unlock. This will be the approach I will talk about the most in this book. I rarely buy shares just to sell them for profit. I now buy shares in established companies that have stable or growing revenues, have a history of profitability and quality dividend yield. I wait for them to come to my price, and I buy them with the intent to hold. But if I subsequently see an opportunity to sell, I will do so. If you look at my trading list at the end of the book, the proportion of dividend income is much higher in this phase. Until the publishing date of this book, there were 23 dividend payments, while 11 completed trades since the start of 2018 were profitable. That gives me a trading record of 76 wins and 9 losses, in addition to quite a few dividend payments. And my record stands at 15 wins and 0 losses since 2017.

I have learnt the following lessons since I started, and I hope to address them with examples as the book goes on. Simply put, what I write below is what I wish I had known when I started, rather than having to learn it through trial and error over time:

1. Define your Strategy. What do you want to achieve, where are you going to invest? What shares / industry segments are you going to trade in? You should have a clear definition of what constitutes a successful trade for you. Review that constantly – I am on Version 5 now.

2. Never enter the stock market unless you have surplus funds in hand. You do not ever want to be in a position where you are in a rush to sell them. Never borrow to invest.

3. Always be focused when the market opens. If anything of significance is going to happen, it will happen in the first five minutes. The rest of the day will most likely follow the pattern.

4. You make your money when you buy the share, not when you sell it. Never rush into buying a share unless it meets all the conditions you have set. It is far, far less painful when you miss an opportunity to buy a share that eventually rose in value than to be stuck with a hastily bought share that has seen its price fallen.

5. Know the shares you want to buy and work out the price you are willing to pay for them. 'Stalk' them every day and let it come down to your price. Never go

chasing it just because it didn't come down to your price.

6. Invest in a share you can live with for life if you are unable to sell it. After that, you can think about selling it.

7. Never regret seeing the share rise after you have sold it for a profit because you did not hold it longer. Know that you have beaten the market. You made your decision based on the information you had at a given point in time and sold in line with your plan. Every time you sell a share for profit, you win.

8. Junk shares have that name for a reason. Avoid them unless you know better.

9. Know your ideal investment and base all your trades on it, or as close as possible to that scenario. For example, my current ideal investment would tick all the following boxes:
   - Constituent of FTSE-100 or FTSE-250.
   - Within an industrial segment that focuses on the essentials of life.
   - Growing revenue for the past five years.
   - Growing profits for the past five years.
   - Growing dividend for the past five years.
   - The balance sheet shows growing or stable cash flows and stable or declining borrowings (Current and Non-Current).
   - The dividend yield is 10% at the current market price.
   - The current market price is close to its 52 Week Low.

- The market price is low due to overall market conditions rather than issues with the company itself.

10. Never pretend you understand the market or that you can predict its behaviour. The market operates in waves that are not determined by you. You just have to learn how to ride them; build a strategy that allows you the best opportunity to get in at the right time and get out at the right time.

11. Buy based on numbers or strategy, never on personal preference. You must never get emotional about investments. For example, I am passionate about aviation, and to me, airlines are the most glamorous business you can be in.

    On the other hand, I have never smoked in my life and do not understand why people would pay to destroy their own lungs and how it's legal for tobacco companies to sell cigarettes.

    But when it comes to business, I rarely buy airline shares, and I have a significant and profitable holding in tobacco shares.

12. Know when to get out and cut your losses. Admittedly it is a lesson I am yet to fully learn and accept. It remains a chink in my own tactics, which I admit to. But it is an important loss-prevention measure to consider. You will live to fight another day.

The book explains all these principles in a bit more detail with real examples from my experience and all that I have learnt. I have also shared the full record of my trading history to date to give more context and to practically demonstrate the outcome of all that I have written here, as they played out in a live environment.

Stock Market – Getting Started

"If you want to invest because you're feeling lucky, walk away now. Your objective from this point on should be to cut luck out as much as possible and beat the odds through tactics."

Before you decide to go into the stock market, let's run through a checklist of things you must consider:

Surplus Funds

While the stock market represents an opportunity to generate a higher return for the funds you will invest, it is, nevertheless, a risk. Therefore, you must ensure that the funds you intend to invest are purely surplus to your requirements. By surplus, I mean you should not need them for any known expense in the foreseeable future.

You absolutely do not want to have a time limit placed upon you to sell your shares when you may need the funds you wish to invest. And, for the sake of your own sanity, please do not borrow money to invest. I emphasise this as strongly as possible because you should not ever feel rushed to sell an investment you have bought. The share price may drop and rise several times before you finally see an opportunity to sell at your target price and profit. Ideally, you should buy a share as if you intend to keep it for life.

"Buy a stock the way you would buy a house. Understand and like it such that you'd be content to own it in the absence of any market" – Warren Buffett

And when the Oracle of Omaha also recommends this approach, it is probably worth bearing in mind. It took me till 2016 to fully understand it.

Do not invest all your savings. And when you start, select a reasonable amount. When I started in FTSE-100, I began with £1,000.

Restrictions to Trading

You may be in a role that prevents you from legally trading, as you may have access to privileged information, which may give you an unfair advantage. If you trade using such information, you may really end up like Gordon Gecko and in jail for 'insider trading'.

These restrictions typically apply to staff working in public accounting firms (as they may have access to financial data yet to be released), regulators and rating companies (as they can influence prices) and any other person who, for one reason or the other, may have access to such information. This is something you must check before you start trading.

You may not be allowed to trade in certain stock markets or certain sectors or not permitted to trade at all. You may also have to obtain permissions for each and every trade you make from your employers or regulator, which restricts and limits the flexibility with which you can operate. For example, you may spot an opportunity but may need to get permission to trade. And by the time you get the clearance, the opportunity has passed.

I stopped trading when I was working in public accounting firms in the UK, simply because of such restrictions, and I did not restart till I moved out and started working for businesses that were not publicly traded (and therefore I had no legal restriction on my ability to trade in shares). At that point, all restrictions were lifted, and I was able to trade with the flexibility and freedom that I consider are essential to be able to trade effectively.

Select your Market

Once you have established that you have the surplus funds available and no restrictions apply to you, select the market you want to trade in. There are online trading platforms that allow you to trade in multiple global stock markets. You can buy shares in the London Stock Exchange and the New York Stock Exchange at the same time.

I would not recommend going global and buying shares in multiple markets, at least not when you are starting out. I certainly do not do that; I stick with London Stock Exchange. That allows me to be more focused on it and keep up with the trends that impact it.

Once again, if you are willing to dedicate more time and research to this, you can expand with time. But when you are starting out, start out slowly and figure out how the process works. Walk before you run! And to my target audience for this book, which is an investor who cannot dedicate a lot of time to this because of a day job, I recommend picking your home stock market as a starting point.

Set up a Trading Account

There are multiple online brokers available where you can open a trading account with access to all major global stock markets. They will most likely require you to prove identification, residency and source of funds as part of their 'Know Your Client and 'Anti Money Laundering' requirements.

I personally use a UK-based online broker with whom I have worked since 2008. I have never felt the need to change it. I pay a fixed amount for every transaction I conduct in addition to any other duties (usually a stamp duty) that applies.

There are generally two popular types of trading accounts that are available to an individual investor:

Margin Account

This account allows you to buy more than the cash you add into your account, with all trades being primarily funded by the broker and your shares being the collateral for the amount you borrow. This is typically used for short-term trading.

For example: Your investment can be £1,000 with a margin requirement of 20%. That means you can buy shares worth up to £5,000 (£1,000 from your account and £4,000 borrowed from the broker). If you buy shares worth £5,000 and sell them for £6,000—your broker will get repaid the first £4,000 with the balance of £2,000 going to your account.

However, if you sell for a loss in the same transaction, for example, if you sell for £4,500, the broker will recover their £4,000, and you will be left with £500.

There may also be situations where you may be required to top up your cash deposit if your share price drops below the margin agreed with your broker. Continuing the example above, if the share value falls below £3,000, then the collateral (your £1,000 deposit and value of shares) is less than the £4,000 you borrowed from the broker). The broker might sell your shares off to protect his or her margin unless you pay in more cash to address the value drop and protect the broker's funds.

My advice on this approach is quite clear: do not touch this account. It breaks one of my golden rules: to always trade on surplus funds and never on borrowed money. Stay with the more conventional cash accounts, explained below.

Pros	Cons
Buying in excess of your own funds available. If a short-term trade works out well, the capital gain will be far higher than what would be possible with your own funds.	• Your risk is not limited to your funds, as you are borrowing from the broker. If the share price drops and you want to hold, you may have to add more funds. • Limited control, as the broker can sell your shares if they drop below a certain threshold to protect themselves.

Cash Accounts

This is my recommended way of trading. You set this trading account up with an amount using surplus funds in line with what suits you, although there will typically be a minimum starting limit. You can buy shares with the amount you have, which means your risk is limited to what you have in the account. You can hold them as long as you like, even if the share is below your purchase price.

Pros	Cons
• Risk limited to funds invested. • Full control on the ability to hold shares, even if the share price drops.	Your gains are limited to the funds. You might make a great transaction that results in a 25% gain but on your own funds. Had it been on a margin account, the gain would have been magnified five times, on a 20% margin account, or ten times with a 10% margin account.

Select your Preferred Industry and Companies

To further simplify your approach, I would strongly recommend picking stocks that fit your risk appetite and approach. At this point, you are developing your strategy and objective. Are you looking for capital gains? If so, you are looking for shares with high volatility and prices that would allow you to benefit from fluctuations.

Or are you looking for stability? If so, this would mean buying shares that you can hold without worrying about selling them and being content with dividend if you are holding them long-term. I have tried both, and I recommend the latter.

There will be hundreds, if not thousands, of companies trading on the stock exchange you chose to trade in. Do not try and focus on all of them. Select the industries you understand best and then, within that, the companies that you prefer. I do not look at or follow more than 20 companies at any given point in time. It allows me to focus my limited time better.

Define your criteria for how you select. For example, I prefer to invest in industries focused on what I describe as 'Essentials of Life' or 'Needs' vs 'Wants'. Therefore, I focus almost exclusively on companies within industry segments such as Oil and Gas, Pharmaceutical, Tobacco, FMGC and Utilities, as they fit my preferred profile.

For example, I limited my focus to Shell (RDSA) and Petrofac (PFC) only within Oil and Gas, as being companies that I considered financially more stable and therefore safer. I used to look at British Petroleum (BP.) as well, but it didn't meet my financial requirements; therefore, I dropped it from my 20 companies.

When I was looking for capital gains in 2017, I focused on PFC. PFC was very volatile at the time due to an almost balanced feed of good news and bad news. They had good financial statements and a credible pipeline of future contracts, but they were also under investigation for bribery. Based on that rationale, I was able to make a few profitable trades on it.

As my approach changed in 2019 towards generating sustainable income rather than pure capital gains, I focused more on RDSA, which had never failed to pay a dividend since World War II. I can hold RDSA for life, so to speak, on dividend return alone, but I can also make a capital gain if the price rises beyond a certain level.

Mock Transactions

This is possibly the dullest part of the process because, by this time, you are raring to go and become the next Warren Buffet. But I would strongly suggest you play with Monopoly money first. Run a few mock transactions and see how they end up.

You should have an idea of what you are trying to do but do test it out first. I would suggest running at least three to five transactions to test your strategy or tactics to see how they play out. Run two or three scenarios (you can because it is not your money yet) and see how they result. Completing those will give you some idea of how the real world might play out. Remember, once you jump into the real world, you cannot undo, reset and try again. I did this for about six months before I started for real.

Now that I have explained the groundwork and you are ready to start, it is time to see how all this plays out in the real world.

Key Points from this Chapter

- ✓ Make sure you have surplus funds to invest with, and there is no foreseeable requirement for them. You do not want to be burdened with the pressure of having a time limit to sell your shares.

- ✓ Your employment or current situation should not place any restrictions on your ability to trade freely.

- ✓ Choose the stock market you will trade in. You may be able to trade in multiple stock exchanges globally, but I recommend staying with one, at least as you start.

- ✓ Open a trading account. There are multiple types, but I recommend a Cash Account over a Margin Account. Invest with what you have and control.

- ✓ While you may have access to the entire market, select your industries of choice, and within that, the companies that meet your requirements. I do not focus on more than 20 companies at any given point in time.

- ✓ As dull as it may seem, conduct mock transactions to test your approach before you actually start to invest with real money.

Defining your Game Plan

"Have a clear game plan before you enter the market and stick to it as much as you can. The market can get tempting and distracting, and that is where it gets dangerous. You need to have a method to steer you clear of any madness."

On the face of it, the process of making money on the stock market is quite simple. You buy some shares at a price you believe is low enough, and you would like to sell them at a price higher than that to make a profit. Some of those shares you buy may pay you a dividend while you hold them. And that is just about it. But what you cannot do is hope to achieve this consistently on judgement, gut feeling or worst of all... advice from an 'expert'!

I will cover the strategies I followed through my career thus far, the pros and cons of each, and then focus more on the current version I have settled on as that has given me some decent results with a strong emphasis on risk minimisation.

1999 to 2004

The Pure Capital Gain Approach

Before I entered the stock market, I completed a six-month analysis of about 16 companies tracking their daily movements to identify their highs and lows. There was no online information available about companies, and financial data would only be available if you could get financial statements in the annual report issued to shareholders.

The Karachi Stock Exchange (at that time anyway) seemed to operate primarily on 'advice and tips' from so-called experts and rumours for individual investors. I was the new kid on the block with data on hand. Even though the data was simply a trend analysis of share movements, it was still more objectively generated information than anyone else had out there. That was an advantage going in.

There was another peculiar element about the trading process the market followed. It was margin-based but allowed a delayed settlement. The trading week was from Monday to Friday, but no matter when you bought the shares, you only had to pay for them on Friday by close of business. And obviously, in the absence of the internet, unless you were sitting with a broker or had access to the stock market trading system, you could not see the real-time movements in shares. So people would just sit there all day, trading away usually on rumours and gossip flying in. I don't think anyone had ever seen a set of financial statements.

That is where I developed my Game Plan V-1. And the rules were as follows:

- I was going to limit my investment to 16 companies that I had been tracking for six months and had analysed for movement trends. I would not look at anything else.
- I was not going to trade on margin but pay for everything in full on Friday at close of business. And I would limit my purchases to the amount already in

my trading account to allow auto-settlement on Friday. That meant my volumes were much smaller compared to other traders.

- I would buy only if the shares were near its low price range based on my trend analysis.
- I was not going to listen to my broker's advice simply because their interest was naturally towards making me buy or sell (as that drove their commission) and not in me holding the investment and making a profit.
- Oh, and I decided to ignore all other expert advice I received as everyone I had consulted told me I would only ever lose money at the stock market, and it was impossible to really make any profits there.

Fortunately, my mother backed my plan and gave me a starting investment of PKR 100,000. And so I went about implementing my big idea.

The first thing I realised was the market was full of big buyers with huge ambitions but not enough money to back them up. These were the margin traders, or 'gamblers' as I liked to think of them. They were my biggest assets, and I remain grateful for their foolishness to this day. These 'gamblers' would place huge orders in the early part of the trading week based on tip-offs or expert advice or broker advice—or 'nonsense' as I liked to call it. Then they would sit in the broker's office all day, hoping for the shares price to rise above their purchase price so they could sell and make their profit.

I had seen in my trend analysis that share prices were, more often than not, at their weekly lowest on a Friday. Now I could see why. My gambling friends would be forced to sell on a Friday, whether they made any profit or not, as they had to settle. And more often than not, I found myself placing my buy orders with full settlement on Friday afternoons. And that is really all I had to do. Wait for Fridays, see if any of my 16 companies were near their 52-week low, and buy whenever that happened.

I do not have the records with me now for that time, but I crossed PKR 200,000 in about a year, doubling my initial investment. No matter what happened, I stuck to my game plan, and it worked every time.

My broker was suspicious as I was training for my Chartered Accountancy in those days with KPMG (FYI – there were no restrictions on trading while working for accounting firms in those days). He was convinced I was using my position in KPMG to obtain inside information to pull of these successful trades one after the other. But that wasn't his problem with me. His only objection was that I was not sharing this 'inside information' with them, which he thought was rather unsportsmanlike of me. He just would not believe that a novice like me could come in and outperform traders who had been doing this for years. I just told him I was not gambling like others, which he did not believe, of course, and remained upset at my selfishness at not sharing 'inside information'.

And just to clarify, before anyone decides to report me to a regulator, I emphasise I was *not* trading on inside information. I was not even part of the external audit team at the time and did not have any access to privileged information, nor did I try to obtain it. Trend analysis was working fine for me, and my dear old gambling traders kept faltering to give me perfect opportunities to buy.

I eventually added PKR 200,000 to my investment base and continued investing. But then I broke one golden rule and did it just one time. I invested on advice and without validation. I remember that cursed company: Fauji Fertilizer Corporation (FFC). It crashed immediately after I bought it.

I walked away from this part of my life in 2001, after being transferred by KPMG to Saudi Arabia with about 20% gain on my overall equity—a far cry from where the gains stood before I invested in FFC. I have never purchased anything on expert advice again.

There was a Part II to this approach, as I reignited my passion for trading and discovered an online account that allowed me to trade in the Karachi Stock Exchange. But that was the least successful part of my trading life as I tried the same approach again to a market that had matured. The settlement terms were different, and I continued my focus on pure trend analysis despite financial information now being more readily available. The world had changed, and I did not; therefore, I paid the price for it.

In short, it was a disaster as I was working with an old model in a new world and effectively gambling like the margin traders I used to look down upon. My only saving grace was that I was not very active so my exposure was limited, and therefore it was not as painful to sell off and walk away in 2004. I had stopped winning, and therefore I had lost interest.

That should have been it for me, which is what I had thought at the time. Because I had at that moment begun to believe that a part-time trader couldn't make money at the stock market. At that point, my stock market days were over.

2004 to 2008
A Self-Imposed Hiatus...

2008 to 2012
Chasing Capital Gains in the London Stock Exchange

I took a four-year hiatus after the painful exit in 2004. But after finding my feet in the UK and settling in, the lure of the stock market was irresistible. And it all simply began with me not being able to figure out what to do with a little bit of money I had saved. I would have liked to put a down payment on a house, but the post-2008 mortgage rules were very tricky, particularly if you were just a UK resident and not a UK citizen (which I was not at the time). I had to look for a different means to invest those funds, and all I knew was the stock market.

After I left public accounting firms and the trading restriction lifted, I began exploring the market, and clearly, the online trading world had advanced quite a lot. All the trends I used to manually and painstakingly maintain were there on a broker's website, as well as financial data that I had never really studied before.

I found myself a trading platform I liked and one that charged reasonably. I settled for Jarvis Investment Management Limited, and I still use their website www.sharedealactive.co.uk for all my trades.

And as before, there had to be some rules. Game Plan V-2 was born:

- I would not limit myself to a certain number of companies but rather keep an eye on top fallers and risers.
- I would buy when a share had a fall in price and got close to or set an all-time low.
- I would focus more on shares with a very low price as there would be less room to fall further, and I could buy high volumes.
- I would just refer to financial data to see if there was any threat to the company's ability to continue in the foreseeable future (Going Concern).

Now that I look at it with hindsight, there were parts of the plan that I do not think were particularly clever. I think it worked well because it was just after the 2008 crash, and the markets were picking up, and I was a bit lucky with the junk shares I bought.

My buying price per share was on average just £1.73 for the 25 transactions I completed, and I only got dividend 8 times in four years. I found myself targeting companies with share prices in pennies, and there were some big returns percentage-wise.

The only clever thing I did was I kept the amounts low, as I knew I was learning again—that one golden rule of mine that you should only invest with surplus funds.

In the end, I made 25 transactions over four years, made a profit twenty times and lost five times. One company ceased trading while I was still holding shares. And that led to me cutting out junk shares from my strategy completely.

2013 to 2017
The Pursuit of Quality Investments

By 2013, I had added a bit more money to the fund I was investing in and began to get uncomfortable with the level of risk I was taking. It was the beginning of the awakening, and this strategy was the beginning of me taking key steps towards my current, far more successful approach.

I prepared an updated set of rules for the launch of Game Plan V-3:

- The objective was to buy with the intent to sell but use dividend as protection if the share had to be held long.
- Investments would be limited to FTSE-100 or FTSE-250 companies only. The focus would be on quality investments and no more junk shares.
- Industries would be limited to those focusing on products and services I considered to be Essentials of Life. Therefore, I created a watchlist of companies I could invest in and gave them all a target price. I would no longer look at all companies—a throwback to my original 1999 strategy.
- Every company must have a history of consistent revenue, profits and dividend payout.
- The dividend must be at least 5% yield based on my purchase price.
- Buying must be when the share drops to near its 52-week low.

I completed 49 transactions in this phase and 45 making a profit. My average buying price increased from £1.73 per share in the previous phase to £14.38 per share. There were also 17 dividend payments in the mix to further prop up the gains. The big loss resulted from becoming too confident about the spikes Petrofac (PFC) was creating and not understanding why it was not following the market trend.

Additionally, this became a slightly more intense approach with a higher number of transactions, and it began to conflict with my work and high travel schedule. The whole premise of my investment approach was that I should be able to do it in addition to my day job. And this approach, while successful, needed more time and research.

I wanted the next reiteration to be more long-term focused, less risky and more reliant on dividend than capital gains. Simply put, an approach I could sustain with the limited time I had available to put towards investments.

2018 Onwards
The Hold-for-Life Approach

In the earlier strategy, I was pursuing shares on which I could make a decent capital gain while protecting myself with dividend in the last version of the strategy. While doing that, there were some instances where, if I got bought the share right, I could end up with dividend that was upwards of 10%. I also wanted to get to a point where I could hold shares without having to sell them just because of the dividend return.

That is when I developed the current version of my strategy – Game Plan V-4:

- The objective now was to buy a share that yields over 10% on the purchase price and meets as many of the safety checks as possible, as discussed in the ***My Ideal Investment*** chapter later in the book.
- A check of financial statements was now mandatory with a focus on revenue, profit, dividend, cash flow and borrowings.
- Identify shares that meet the high-dividend criteria, define the ideal price that gets the required yield, and then let the shares come to that price. I would not chase shares; I would set my target price for all companies I followed and let them come to me
- The ideal price should still be near the 52-week low. This is one rule that has not changed since 1999!
- The old rule of only investing in a company trading in Essentials of Life and being part of FTSE-100 or FTSE-250 still applied.
- Check the recent news for the company to see if there is anything that could suggest a company-specific risk not related to the market.
- Buy with the intent to hold for life unless the capital gain exceeds two years dividend. Then I would sell.
- Any deviation from this strategy must have a very good reason. My IAG trade in May 2020 was the only one outside this strategy, but the circumstances were too good and obvious to resist. I backed my aviation knowledge over these rules for once.

The record for this strategy stands at 11 profitable trades and no losses. And there hasn't been a loss-making trade since 2017. The average buying price increased further from £14.38 per share to £16.54 as I pursued higher-quality investments. I have shares in the red, but the intention was to generate a high dividend yield, which they still provide. The number of transactions I carry out per year has dropped significantly. I have received dividend 23 times in this period.

My watchlist is more focused and shorter, and my hold time is intentionally higher as opposed to being stuck with shares that do not pay back.

This is the strategy where I feel safer and secure. I can now build towards my next reiteration, which is simply to add to this approach and build an income-per-day approach. My ultimate ambition now is that my investments should become my pension and pay for my life in case (for some reason that I cannot imagine now) I ever choose to retire and take up gardening or golf!

Key Points from this Chapter

- ✓ Define your set of rules on how you will handle the market. Write them down and then stick to them no matter how tempting the market gets.
- ✓ Key Rule 1 – Buy as if you intend to hold for life, and then look to sell.
- ✓ Key Rule 2 – Buy good companies that are available at a good price due to a momentary drop in value.
- ✓ Key Rule 2 – Never ignore the financial statements. Look at them before you buy.
- ✓ Key Rule 3 – Check the recent news about the company as part of your assessment.
- ✓ Key Rule 4 – It is not just about capital gains; focus on dividends as well since they can be a safe source of income and a very decent return on investment.

Funding your Investments

"Your ability to hold the investment long is directly proportional to your likelihood of success."

Investment in a stock market should never be seen as a short-term play, even if your intention is exactly that. No matter what your game plan is and what your objectives are, you have to be cognisant of the fact that you are ultimately trying to predict an outcome that may or may not happen. Alternatively, it may happen much later than you expect. And the timeline of that is something you should not pretend to know or control. There are just far too many variables and uncertainties in play, and their impact on how the market reacts is sometimes based on human sentiments rather than facts (Refer to the ***'A Market you do not Control'*** chapter).

One of the fundamental rules of investing is that an investor who buys long-term almost always has more success than an investor who plays short-term. Your ability to hold on to an investment and see out the tremors in its price over time just allows you more time to achieve your objective. You should never find yourself in a situation where you are rushed to liquidate the investment because you need the funds. In my view, ability and intent to hold separate the serious investors from casual traders, whom I respectfully can only describe as gamblers.

Investments in quality shares (if properly done) are simply a cleverer form of savings; only here, the savings can grow in value if you play it right, and the reward will be higher than any bank account can offer.

To spell this out again (for more emphasis), savings for the purpose of investment in the stock market means an amount that you currently have and which is in surplus of what you need right now or in the foreseeable future.

Your investment plan should be based on an amount you believe you can comfortably set aside periodically, after allowing for your costs of living and perhaps a portion of savings dedicated to cover an emergency liquid reserve. The rest of it should go towards your broader saving plan, and that could be based either entirely on shares, on any other form of investment, or a blend of multiple investments. As long as all of it is not sitting in a bank account, earning you next to nothing.

Holding a large balance in a deposit with a bank is effectively a waste of money as you are losing out on the potential of its earning capability, and it might just be losing value due to inflation. This is generally defined as the Time Value of Money.

My personal approach to funding my stock market investment is as below, and while it may seem simple, remarkably few people I have come across seem to ever have a credible savings and investment plan:

1. Start with what you expect to earn every month. Let's say the amount you receive as your salary or your Earnings.

2. Identify and budget for what you need to spend every month. Then add 20 per cent to it. This is the amount you retain but never invest this amount. Deduct this amount from your Earnings to arrive at your Savings.
3. Move the Savings amount to a dedicated savings pool, ideally in a different bank account. This should happen as soon as you have received your income and before you start spending. ***The golden rule is that you always save before you spend***.
4. Project any medium- to long-term spending requirements and put that money aside as well, separately from your Savings balance to identify Surplus.
5. From the amount you identify as your Surplus, identify where you want to invest it. If it is in the stock market, then allocate an amount to the stock market fund and move it to your trading account pool.
6. Wait for the right opportunity to buy, and then buy it outright. I do not recommend buying on margin.

To put this as a simple example, see the table below, and I'll discuss it further in the chapter:

Income per Month (Net After Tax) – Earnings		**£4,000**
Rent / Mortgage	£1,000	
Food, Grocery and General	£1,000	
Others	£500	
Expenses		**(£2,500)**
20% Buffer on Expenses		**(£500)**
Savings		**£2,000**
Allocation for Medium- to Long-Term Commitments		**(£500)**
Surplus – Allocated to Investments		**£1,500**

If I were to allow a conservative 10% return on investment on your investments, based on £1,500 saved every month, it would allow you to generate an extra £975 per year. And that you can do just with dividends. Add capital gains to it; that will inevitably arise if you buy right, you could easily double that. No bank can ever match that level of profitability!

Surplus Funds

Invest only using what you consider as surplus from your savings. I want to distinguish between savings and surplus. Savings are what is left over after you have met your cost of living, but then you may have a commitment coming up shortly for which you may need those funds.

Surplus Funds are savings, after allowing for any foreseeable future commitments—let's say for a year. This is just excess money you do not need and are not quite sure what to do with. It is a very fortunate position to be in. And this is what you need to make work in your favour.

This money can be left lying in a bank earning minimal interest, or you can invest it, and since we are here talking about shares, that is an investment option where I suggest you at least put some portion of it towards.

Investing with surplus funds allows you to buy without the fear of having to sell immediately. You are now investing with a long-term horizon in mind and, therefore, will assess the performance of a share over a long-term basis.

Good companies may have short-term fluctuations but are sustainable with their performance regardless of most economic and global changes that cause tremors in the market. They usually can do well over a longer run. This gives you ample time to generate dividend income, and you also have the option to wait for the right price before you sell for a capital gain.

In reality, this approach might end up being a short-term investment if you get the desired gain quickly, but the mindset that you apply in your approach to buying must always be long-term.

I can say from experience that I have found myself selling off my 'long-term' investments profitably in the short- to medium-term quite frequently. In contrast, when I was more inclined to buy 'short-term' investments to seek capital gains, I got stuck with quite a few for a 'long-term'. Fortunately, after learning the hard way and revising my strategy, I always made sure I always bought a 'share for life' and learnt that holding long-term can be very rewarding as well.

Buy Outright

When you are investing using your surplus funds, then, unless you happen to be extremely well off, there is the temptation to buy a high volume of shares on margin. As explained earlier, this is entirely possible, and you only pay for a percentage of the value of the shares you buy. But while you own the reward, the increased risk is also entirely yours.

A sharp drop in value may require you to top up the amount you have invested to cover the margin gap. And that may result in you having to spend more than your surplus. And when you have to go beyond your surplus to invest, the stock market starts to become a very dangerous world.

That is not an approach I recommend. Always buy the shares you want outright and limit the risk to your surplus. The reward may be limited, but it will still be yours. It may limit the volume of shares you can buy, but you remain in control. You can then reinvest your gains and future surplus and grow your buying capability organically. Good things come to those who wait.

Key Points from this Chapter

- ✓ Always invest in the stock market with a long-term mindset.
- ✓ Invest with funds that you consider are surplus to your needs. That will allow you to hold shares for a longer term.
- ✓ Surplus funds = Savings minus funds required for known commitments over the next year.
- ✓ Save before you spend—that is a golden rule you should apply regardless of whether you choose to invest or not.
- ✓ Buy shares outright and not on margin. That way, you limit your risk to your surplus and retain the reward. Buying on margin increases the reward but also the risk, which may require you to fund the investment beyond your surplus funds.

Learn to Read the Accounts

"Financial statements are the language of business. Learn to read them, at least the parts that matter most."

Before you decide to buy into any company, no matter how good the price looks or the positivity of news regarding its future prospects seem, it is always a good idea to look into the numbers behind that company—its financial statements. That is the best source of its true performance history. And because you are looking to invest in a listed company, the financial data available is quite credible, independently audited, and published at quarterly and half-yearly intervals and on an annual basis.

I have a bit of an advantage here as I am a Chartered Accountant, so I was trained on IFRS to prepare, interpret and analyse financial statements. However, to expect anyone, including me, to fully examine the document in detail is a daunting task. Since the fundamental idea of this book was to keep things as simple as possible, let us stick to the very basic data that I would recommend you review from any company's financial statements before you decide to buy or not.

When I began my career, it was not that easy to find financial statements online, and therefore it was practically impossible to get my hands on them to review instantly when there was an opportunity to buy shares in a particular company.

Now as it stands, my online brokerage firm has all key aspects of all companies' financial statements for the last five years, as well as interim results available at the click of a button. I can also go to any company's website to find their financial statements and look at them in as much detail as I like.

Here are the minimum aspects of the financial statements that I would recommend you focus on:

Income Statement

Revenue

Revenue is simply the amount of income generated by a business in a defined period, ideally a year. I like to analyse it for the last five years and what I am looking for is growth or (at least) stability year on year. This gives me assurance that the company has longevity and is a good indicator of not only its current business being stable but also a good basis to assess the demand for its products or services in the near future.

On occasion, I will check if all the revenue is from continuing operations and not of a 'one-off' nature. This can sometimes be misleading, particularly if you rely on summarised data and not the main financial statements. I would suggest a more thorough read of the financial statements in this regard if it is a company you are not familiar with or looking at for the first time.

Profit (Gross and Net)

Ultimately, revenue does not mean much if there is no or inadequate profitability at the end of it all. The more important number to look at is Net Profit, as that is the end result. And nothing is more reassuring than a growing trend of Revenue combined with growing Net Profit.

Do check Gross Profit though or Operating Profit. It shows the core strength of the company's operations. Typically, you would expect a similar trend to Revenue and Net Profit, but a deviation may indicate the impact of one-off activities.

For example, I used to invest in Whitbread (WTB) once, when I was pursuing pure capital gain as a strategy. Please review their financial statements summary below:

Whitbread (WTB)			
Year End	**Revenue**	**Gross Profit**	**Pre-Tax Net Profit**
03 March 2016	£ 2,911 M	£ 524 M	£ 488 M
02 March 2017	£ 3,106 M	£ 549 M	£ 515 M
01 March 2018	£ 2,007 M	£ 465 M	£ 427 M
28 Feb 2019	£ 2,049 M	£ 366 M	£ 218 M
27 Feb 2020	£ 2,071 M	£ 409 M	£ 280 M

The pattern of growth deviates in 2018 with a significant drop in Revenue, while the Gross Profit drops as well as a drop in Pre-Tax Net Profit. However, this was not as alarming as it might appear. WTB sold its Costa Coffee brand in 2018, and there was a one-off gain of an additional £ 3.5 billion as a result. However, it did change the dynamics of the business and its profitability margins.

The purpose of this example is to highlight that changes in patterns may have underlying, one-off reasons that become apparent by going a level deeper in the financial statements to gain a full understanding before deciding to invest. For the record, WTB was one of my preferred shares for capital gain, but its rather low dividend ratio eventually caused its appeal to dwindle for me, particularly when I switched to my current approach to investing.

Dividend

Since I now base my investment decisions primarily on dividend yield, I always look for total dividend paid over five years and a growth trend within that area. I then compare it to the market price to see whether it meets my yield requirement of 10% plus.

A growing pattern of dividend is reassuring. Companies that continue to give dividend during the turbulent COVID era of 2020-2021 are even more reassuring as to me that is an indicator of a company having immense confidence in the sustainability of its business. This, of course, is checked with the Income Statement and Balance Sheet trends, which should also reflect that positivity.

Balance Sheet

Cash and Cash Equivalents

While holding excess liquidity is not the best approach to business, a Balance Sheet that shows stable or growth in Cash and Cash Equivalents while meeting all my Income Statement requirements is rather reassuring. It indicates

to me that the company has a bit of self-reliance and an ability to deal with surprises that inevitably show up.
I might run through the Statement of Cash Flows just to get a feel for how the cash is being generated and spent to back up the Balance Sheet number. What I typically look out for are major sources of inflows and outflows. For example, if cash is increasing due to an increase in borrowing, then that would impact my assessment.

Borrowings (Current and Non-Current)

I look for similar reassurance while reviewing borrowings (or 'leverage' as it is referred to commonly). A growing pattern of borrowings does not appeal to me unless I can see a good reason for it in the business performance. I prefer growth in Capital or Equity rather than an increase in borrowings. I like to see stability or, ideally, a decline in borrowings over a five-year period.

There is, of course, a lot more detail you can review, such as Earning per Share ratios and Price Equity ratios (both covered in the chapter ***My Ideal Investment***), along with Debt Equity ratios and the details behind each and every figure of the financial statements. Still, if we stick to the objective of simplicity in this book, this is what I would recommend as a minimum. And this is what I largely use before pressing the button to buy, or indeed walking away from what may (on the face of it) look like a fabulous opportunity.

Key Points from this Chapter

- ✓ Learn to read financial statements and know the key information to look for to analyse. Look at published financial statements or summaries derived from them. All this is available quite easily online.

- ✓ In the Income Statement section, analyse trends in Revenue, Gross Profit and Net Profit. Watch out for one-off events and when you see any deviations from trends, explore the reason. Growth trends suggest stability and demand for the products or services the company sells.

- ✓ Analyse Dividend payout trends as they indicate a company's confidence in its sustainability.

- ✓ In the Balance Sheet, analyse trends of growth or declines in Cash and Cash Equivalents and Borrowings (Current and Non-Current).

You Make Money when you Buy

"You make your money when you buy the share, not when you sell it. Never rush into buying a share unless it meets all the conditions you have set."

The simple rule of the stock market is you buy low, and you sell high. And no matter how complicated you make your investment approach, this golden rule always stands. Therefore, with that rule firmly in mind, how you buy matters more than anything else. It is the only part of the investment you control. Because once you have bought a share at the right price and the right time, selling is easy!

Buying is the absolute key to success in this business. And buying at the right price can be an incredibly frustrating process that requires a lot of patience. I relate the process of buying at the right price to fishing. You pick the perfect fishing spot, set the right bait, and throw in the line. Then you wait for it, endlessly at times, till the fish bites. If it does not work, then you come back the next day and try again. And if you persist long enough, you will get the perfect catch.

That is also how you buy shares. You work out the price that suits you for each share you are interested in, then place an order to buy at that price whenever the share is near enough, like a bait. Then you wait for it patiently. And every day, you set your 'bait' till either you buy the shares, or they elude you and the price rises without you being able to buy it. And then you start all over again till you get your perfect buy.

For me, not being able to buy a share that was so close to my target price is fine. It can get very frustrating and annoying, but I can live with that. The cash still remains in my hand, and I live to fight tomorrow with another idea. My options remain available. <u>You never chase a share if it does not come to your price.</u>

Always remember that no matter how frustrating it gets when you miss out on a purchase, it does not even come close to the grief you will feel being stuck with a share that falls well below the price you purchased. When you miss a purchase, you have an option to do something else tomorrow.

But if you have purchased in a rush and are stuck with a share that is in the red; you have no options. I would happily miss out on buying a share any day, just to avoid being stuck with poorly purchased shares again. I can, unfortunately, say that from experience, having spent nearly a decade holding PVCS!

I can give you examples of where I have literally stalked a share for weeks waiting for it to drop to the price I was willing to pay. Each day I set up a buy order in the morning only to see the share price come close but not low enough.

The IAG purchase in May 2020 is a classic example, and I will take you through it. As I mentioned before, I do not like investing in certain companies, and airlines are one of them. I have dabbled in them on occasions when I see an opportunity for a pure capital gain, and that is simply because I understand that business far better than others.

Background

COVID-19 had just gone past its peak in May 2020, with numbers starting to show some stability. I already knew airlines and anything to do with commercial aviation would suffer quite badly for the next two to three years, as all business models were effectively decimated.

But summer was on the horizon, and discussions were going on within the political circles of power to start reopening travel corridors to allow people, particularly in Europe, to take their holidays.

Rationale

Of all the airline options I could see available to me, I thought IAG was the safest one. They represented three flag carriers and were, in my view, the least likely to shut down. But I also knew any investment in IAG was not going to give a dividend return for years, and the Group was going to make massive losses for a while. But with the travel restrictions likely to ease, I expected the market sentiment to give IAG a short-term boost. And I wanted to benefit from that jump when it happened.

Tactic

As I was consciously planning to break a number of my own rules as an exception, I wanted to be extra vigilant. IAG was hovering just over the £2.00 mark. I decided that I would only buy if it came down to £1.90. I began setting up buy orders every day at £1.90. It was a bit frustrating, as it would drop price every day, but not enough. I recall once missing it by 1.5p. It was very tempting to increase my limit and just buy, but I resisted. And it was only because of my past experience that I was able to resist.

Result

After a series of unfulfilled buy orders (and there is no charge for buy orders that are not fulfilled), IAG's share price finally dropped just enough to scrape my target price of £1.90 on Thursday – 22 May 2020 and I was in business.

Friday – 23 May 2020 was a bank holiday. There were more discussions on resuming travel by June 2020 over the weekend.

On Monday – 26 May 2020, the market opened on a positive note, and IAG jumped. I set my ambitious price of £2.50, eventually lowering it to £2.34 and sold them all. That meant that my weeks of frustration to buy IAG shares at the right price were rewarded with an instantaneous reward of a 23% gain in one working day.

Hence, the moral of this story is that your probability of success is far greater if you put in some serious effort in buying, no matter how frustrating it gets. Here are some steps to follow:

Know your Ideal Investment

There is a full chapter dedicated to this. Have your list of companies researched, so you are focused and tracking them regularly. I have never focused on more than 20 companies at a time.

Know your Buying Price

For all the companies on your list, have a clear buying price that is based on earlier analysis and reflects your business case to buy. This could be based on performance, dividend yield and / or market price history.

Knowing your price in advance is therefore very important. You buy when the share comes to your price and not the price it is at. Review your prices regularly to allow for a change in market and company circumstances.

If you are looking at a company outside your list (as in my IAG example), do additional research and have a clear reason and understanding of your rationale for this purchase.

Lay your Trap and Wait... and Repeat!

When the price of a selected share is close to your threshold, start setting a buy order with a limit. There should be no charge for that unless the order is fulfilled. And this is the frustrating part. You have to set these orders daily (unless your broker allows you to place a long-term order with a limit). And then just wait and wait for the share price to drop to your level.

Be stubbornly resolute with this and never get tempted to increase your price, at least not without good reason and analysis. The share price has to come to your target. The moment you buy, you lose control. Therefore buy it only when you know it is at a price that meets your business case.

Why this Approach?

You are in control of your destiny until the moment you buy the share. From that point, the share price controls you, and you are just a passenger. My approach is based on a preference of setting a price that is aggressively low (but not entirely impossible) based on a given set of circumstances, and I am prepared to miss out on the purchase if the price does not drop to my liking.

If you persist with it over time and keep placing aggressive buy orders, then the share might just scrape your price and allow you to buy before it corrects itself and heads upwards. And then you have your gain.

If you fail to buy, you live to try again and again. Or you can opt for a different share. That, I believe, is a far better situation to be in than buying at market price above your target price because it may drop further. I repeat, I would rather miss out on an opportunity to buy than be stuck with a bad investment I cannot sell off for a gain. And once you have bought right, selling will take care of itself.

Whenever I feel impatient, I just think of PVCS. I purchased it on 27 October 2009 for £0.72 and finally sold it for £0.25 on 02 August 2019. Ten years is a lot of time to think about what else I could have done. That is a decade of my life wasted if I do not learn from it!

Key Points from this Chapter

- ✓ You make your money when you buy, not when you sell. Buying is the skilful part of trading on the stock exchange, while selling is just an administrative function where you either reap the rewards or bear the brunt of the purchase you made.

- ✓ Know the companies you want to buy shares in, know the price you are prepared to pay for them, and then you wait for them to come to your price.

- ✓ It is far better to miss the opportunity to buy a share at the wrong price than to be stuck with an investment in the red after you have bought it. You live to fight again in case you were unable to buy on a day.

- ✓ Prepare to deal with the frustration of not getting the share you want at your price. Patience is the key, as your plan will only work if implemented on your terms.

The Pain of a Profitable Sale

"Your objective for any trade is to meet your business case for the investment, which is your target profit margin either through gain, dividends or a combination of both. Once you have achieved that, you have beaten the market. Learn to live with that should the share rocket up immediately after you have sold, as it is going to happen and it is going to hurt."

There have been times where I have felt that when I buy shares of a company, I inadvertently cast an evil spell on its share price, and the entire world just waits for me to exit so that the spell can be broken, and the share price can rise freely once again. I have waited for months on end for the share price to hit a reasonable return so I can finally exit with a gain, only to feel like an absolute idiot when it shoots up like never before once I have finally sold it. The sense of triumph of making that gain then feels somewhat qualified, as while you have made your target profit, there was potential to make so much more if only you could have seen the future.

As a tragic example, I would like to take you through my 2018 trade in United Utilities (UU), which represented my relaunch as the first investment of my new strategy, targeting a dividend of around 5% while waiting for it to give me a return of 10% on the purchase price.

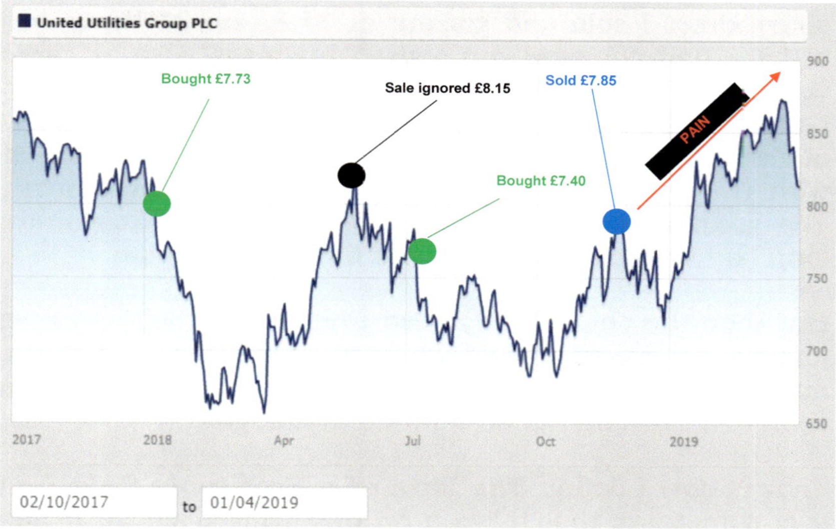

www.youinvest.co.uk

After monitoring it for a while, I was comfortable buying it when the price dropped to £7.73 on 10 January 2018. My target selling price would have been £8.50. The plan seemed to work quite well as the price rose up to £8.15 by May 2018, and I felt confident enough not to sell and wait for dividend coming up in August or a higher gain, whatever came first. Either way, it was looking good.

However, the price did not rise towards my target and, in fact, dropped below my cost price. I began to feel a little edgy, but the upcoming dividend of 28p per share was reassuring. I decided to add to my investment and bought more shares at £7.40 on 10 July 2018, lowering my breakeven costs. But the price just kept dropping further, which was a little concerning. However, its strong dividend prospects kept me confident. At that point, I decided to revise my business case and change my target return from 10% to 5%.

The price eventually rose in November, and (after another sharp drop) I sold and got out at £7.83 on 21 November 2018. I had achieved my revised business case as there was a decent profit, and I had taken a nice dividend payment due to the extended hold. From a tactical point of view, it was a definite trading win. I felt rather pleased with the outcome of my first 'new strategy' investment. The great new idea of holding a dividend-backed share long had worked more or less in line with the plan.

But then the share price, freed from my 'curse', just rose and rose. I asked myself whether I should celebrate the success of the gain or beat myself up for bailing out too soon and missing out on a much higher gain.

That is how I define ***The Pain of a Profitable Sale,*** and it is something that takes a bit of getting used to. It has nothing to do with the methodology of investment that I have covered in the book, but I do not want this inevitable occurrence to distract you and lead to a reactive change in your approach. Your mission for every trade is simply to achieve your pre-defined objective. Whenever you do that, remember you beat the market against the odds, and you still win.

Here is some non-emotive and logical context to this, which is the only way to assess investments. You make a decision to sell based on the information you have on hand at a given moment in time. You cannot see the future. In the example above, I had originally planned to sell for £8.50, but the share price spent a considerable amount of time below my purchase price. Despite my second purchase at a lower price, the price continued to drop. That was the information I had on hand to work with at the time.

I had secured my primary dividend, seen the share go past my breakeven price after a long time, and I had already noted a new trade opportunity developing (I purchased SSE on 03 December 2018). Based on that information on hand at the time, I made the decision to sell. I could not see the future. Now, what happened later made the decision look bad in hindsight. But then hindsight is a perfect science.

I have learnt with time not to let that bother me; well, not as much as it did before anyway. Because every now and then, you do end up making a sale at the peak of the share's price, and then the share drops again. And then you feel like a star!

The Royal Dutch Shell (RDSA) story below is one example where occasionally you get to realise that sticking to a plan and getting out as planned is a good idea.

[*www.youinvest.co.uk*](http://www.youinvest.co.uk)

I purchased RDSA at the peak of the COVID-19 crisis when the world was locking down, so the price of £12.43

was extraordinarily low and a fabulous price under normal circumstances. I backed an eventual recovery and Shell's ability to pay a dividend to give me a decent quarterly return if I got stuck with it.

The price bounced back very quickly, so the share stayed in profit for most of the time I held it. I set myself an ambitious 25% return target and decided to wait it out till that happened. I let go of two opportunities to sell at £15 (as the dividend return was expected to be very good) but then had to revise my plan once the dividend was cut down by the company due to the impact of COVID-19. I settled on a revised selling price of £14. It touched that price finally on 25 November 2020, just after going ex-dividend, and I sold at the day's peak price.

Unlike the previous example, here, the share price dropped immediately after I sold. No such pain here, just a win. Though I could have sold them for £15 earlier, you decide based on the facts you know and understand on the day. Here, even hindsight showed that the decision to sell was a good one. But I have learnt to ignore hindsight and back the methodology.

That is the main message I want to give in the chapter. Your decision to sell is based on information available at any given point in time, and if you sell and make a profit based on that, you have succeeded. Ignore what happens after that and move on to the next one. You need to focus on finding your next victory rather than dwell on what might have been. It's all okay as long as you win!

Key Points from this Chapter

- ✓ Every trade you enter is based on a business case to generate a certain percentage of return on investment, either on an annual basis through dividend or by a capital gain through sale. Or maybe a combination of both, as in my case.

- ✓ You review the performance of each transaction and make a decision to sell or retain based on the circumstances you face and the information you have available to you at any given point in time. And then you make a decision that hopefully makes you a gain.

- ✓ Once you have made the sale and recorded a desired gain, you have met your objective. What the share does after this is beyond your control, and based on information that was probably not available at the time, you decided to sell. Do not let that bother you if you achieved your business case return on investment. Focus on the next trade.

They are called Junk Shares for a Reason

"There is no such thing as a Rock Bottom price."

In my simple world of investment, a junk share is associated with a company that is not doing well financially. Its future prospects are bleak; it is consistently making losses and does not pay any dividend. The share price is typically very low; for me, that usually means below £0.25, and currently, it is near or at its lowest price across a 52-week range.

There is no logical reason to invest long-term in such a company based on performance, so all one can really hope for or hypothesise is that buying shares in such a company at the perceived rock-bottom price could result in a nice gain should the share price spike up for any reason, whether it is rational or otherwise. And even the slightest spike can result in a nice gain (as you would have a high volume in hand due to its very low price).

You have to bear in mind that the share price of such companies is low for a very good reason. And there is never a lowest possible price you can buy them at, as that ultimate rock bottom is zero.

While that is in contrast to my current principles on investing, it represents a potential opportunity. But you really need to know a lot about the company you are 'betting' (I cannot call it investing) on to have some ability to assess its prospects to rise.

When I first decided to include this chapter in my book, I planned to absolutely shoot this approach down, hence the title. I wanted to encourage everyone to avoid this tactic as it is high risk and effectively can be a wild gamble if you are a part-time investor—my target audience for this book. However, upon reflection, I have decided to present a balanced approach and then shoot it down with a couple of exceptions.

Junk shares have this name for a reason, and they seem to be very adept at finding ways of dropping lower than any price you ever thought was rock bottom. Avoid them unless you know better.

If you look at my initial investments in 2008, I applied the logic that every share must have a rock-bottom price. And if I could get a share at that price, there would eventually be a slight upward spike if I waited long enough, and I would get my gain. That is where it became a bit hit and miss.

The biggest weakness in the strategy was not understanding the business or the industry and just hoping that whatever I had bought was indeed at what I considered a rock-bottom price, based on a simple trend analysis across the last 52 weeks. I would also hope that the company would not shut down, at least not before spiking up once to allow me to sell. In hindsight, it was not the brightest idea, but I was testing the waters, so not putting in large amounts.

I classify the following transactions as my junk share deals:

Purchase Date	Sale Date	Share	Buying Price / Share	Selling Price / Share	Gain / (Loss)
16 December 2008	06 January 2009	ORE	£0.07	£0.08	£0.01
Rationale	Aricom was a struggling iron-ore producer that was eventually acquired in April 2009 by another company. My bet was simply based on it being at an all-time low price at the time, confident in my belief that it would not fall any further. As it turned out, I simply got lucky, and it went up by a penny to allow me to get out with a profit. Did I fully know what I was getting into? Definitely not! I just kept my investment value low, volume high and hoped that it might just go up if I buy low enough. And it did. I felt quite clever at the time and decided I was onto something, and this approach might be it.				
19 December 2008	12 January 2009	MEC	£0.01	£0.02	£0.01
Rationale	Mecom was a newspaper publishing group that began to see its revenues go down and share price struggling, presumably as online content became more readily available. I knew that was the case and did not expect it to be a long-term investment. But I applied the same old logic. It was at an all-time low price, and surely the share would not go below 1p. Luckily for me, it rose to 2p after four months, and I got put feeling a bit clever again. I figured I had this all worked out.				
10 October 2010	03 April 2014	YELL	£0.15	Written Off	-£0.15
Rationale	After the success of the previous two junk share bets and a few less 'junky' trades, I decided to go a little bigger with the Yell Group. They published the famous Yellow Pages and were now moving online as well. But the numbers were not that great and declining. Hence the low share price. I recall getting an opportunity to sell it once when it shot up, and I felt a bit too brave perhaps and did not sell it, and instead looked for a bigger gain. The success of the past two transactions had made me a little too overconfident. As it turned out, the price dropped once and for all and then never recovered. I held it even at a low price in the hope of recovery and perhaps stubbornly to not take the first-ever loss. By 2014, the shares were taken off the stock market and valued at zero. And that ended my desire to ever go for a junk share again. If you do not know the industry inside out, do not bet on it.				

Now that was the demotivating part of the story. This went a long way in forming my current approach of investing long-term and in high-dividend-yielding, profitable companies classified as 'Needs'. But I did venture into similar territory again in 2020 at the peak of the coronavirus epidemic. And while strictly speaking, I would not call it a junk share transaction; it is based on the same logic, so it fits well here. The only difference was that this time I knew the industry very well and backed my knowledge to predict the increase in share price.

This is a transaction I have discussed in the chapter ***You Make Money When You Buy***, but I want to cover it again just to give a more balanced view on circumstances where you might just be able to make a leap into junk shares or equivalent work well.

At the peak of the COVID-19 outbreak in March 2020, airline stocks took a massive hammering. Given the circumstances, it was a terrible investment. And I stand by my statement that one should never invest in an airline as a long-term investment as they are just an inherently bad business to be in. However, IAG (British Airways + Iberia + Aer Lingus + Vueling) represents three flag carriers and a low-cost airline. I do not think it can shut down as they are too critical to their home countries.

While the price did not initially drop to junk levels, it did drop significantly as the world shut down for aviation. It dropped from its 2020 peak of £6.71 to below £2.00. Not quite junk levels, but given the circumstances, it was heading there rapidly.

The opportunity was simply the imminent announcements that post-lockdown, the summer of 2020 would see a return to normal travel. While I did not expect any real long-term improvement in airline performance, that imminent announcement seemed like a certain trigger for a share price spike.

I bought IAG on 22 May 2020 for £1.90. The announcement of travel restrictions lifting came over the weekend, and the share price shot up on 26 May 2020. I sold for £2.33—an instant gain of 23%. Had I held a bit longer, I would have sold for over £3.00, but that is hindsight.

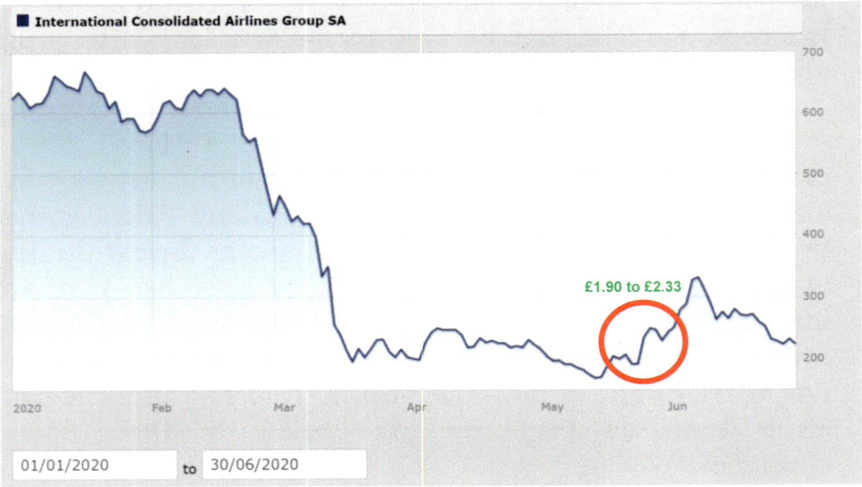

www.youinvest.co.uk

A second opportunity also presented itself later in the year, when the share price went as low as £0.86, but I had set my target price at £0.85 with the expectation that the price would double within six months. I stuck to my rule of not budging from my target price, but that is hindsight once again, and hindsight is a perfect science.

Had I managed to buy it, I would have sold it for more than £2.00 within five months. I would probably not dare try this with any other industry, though.

The reason why I discussed IAG again is to give the junk shares approach a bit of context. In general, my advice is to avoid it completely. Stick with the long-term investment approach, and you will make money. The only exception that I now allow myself occasionally is airlines. And that is because I have worked 17 years in the industry and back myself to be able to predict, under certain circumstances, the future outcome of the share price based on the industry outlook.

If you want to bet (I insist it is not investment) on an industry, do so with low amounts to test yourself and only when you know an industry well enough. This is where perhaps you can really make very large profits, but if it goes wrong, you will lose big.

May the odds be in your favour!

Key Points from this Chapter

- ✓ Buying junk shares is not an investment; it is gambling. It is not how the stock market was intended to be used.

- ✓ If you buy poor-performing companies at their all-time low price, there is probably a very good reason why they are there. You are simply hoping that it might spike up a little bit to allow you to get out with a profit. But it can go the other way.

- ✓ The only real rock bottom is zero. If you bet on junk shares long enough, you will learn that the hard way.

- ✓ The only cautious exception I dare to suggest is betting on an industry that you know very well. And you should know it well enough to predict the near future to a certain extent. Even then, you are simply improving your odds.

- ✓ If you choose to take this approach, start with very low amounts. This can make you large gains but also wipe you out quickly.

- ✓ Or... just don't go for it. It is Very High Risk! Focus on investing and not gambling.

My Ideal Investment

"Never buy shares to sell and make a gain, buy them with the intent to hold, and then look to sell."

I consider this chapter to be the most important one in this book. *If you read nothing else from what I have written, do take some time to understand the points I make here.*

Having gone through multiple reiterations of my approach to investment and what I want to invest in, and perhaps having lost a bit of an appetite for risk, I began the search for investments that I could live with without having to worry about ever having to sell them. And the obvious starting point for me was the dividend that the company pays over a year.

I began examining all companies, initially on FTSE-100 and then added to them those on FTSE-250. I was surprised to find that there were quite a few options out there where dividend yields – if the share was purchased at the right market price – were well above 5% on the buying price. I was surprised to find options with up to and over 10% dividend yield, and for me, that is a level where I could completely stop worrying about whether the share price goes up or down, as my return on investment remains 10%.

However, I also found out that high dividend may not always be an indicator of a good company, as some companies were simply maintaining a high dividend to remain attractive despite their financial performance not being quite strong enough to justify such returns, or there were companies where the dividend was simply high because their share price had crashed for a good reason—and the dividend was not going to last long.

From that point on, my quest became to find a set of companies that were financially sound over a long period and which had been issuing a solid dividend for that duration. And to find my perfect investment company, I had to first define what exactly that meant.

The guidelines below define my absolute perfect investment. I cannot recall any company ever meeting every possible requirement to perfection, but what I do know is that when I invest as close as possible to these guidelines, I have always made a gain. What you read below is one of the key takeaways from this book:

Constituent of the FTSE-100 or FTSE-250 (or the Primary Index of any Stock Exchange you opt for)

There are approximately 2,600 companies listed on the London Stock Exchange and about 41,000 listed across all stock markets globally. I cannot keep an eye on all of them, and not all of them represent a good or safe investment.

A company that qualifies to be listed on FTSE-100 or even FTSE-250 is more likely to have longevity and the advantage of scale. It would have demonstrated sustainability to get to where it is. That forms the first check on my safety list. I have invested in companies outside these indices in the past, but I have found that it is safer and more rewarding to stay within a major index in the last decade. This can be any primary stock market index in the world, but I focus on FTSE-100 and FTSE-250. I haven't strayed outside this limit for years.

Therefore, unless you have the time and availability of resources to identify a lesser-known, high-quality stock, I suggest you start off with companies within a major index, learn and let your own experience grow and then decide where to go next.

Every stock exchange has a primary index or a set of primary indices that focus on its leading listed companies and are considered a measure of market performance. The London Stock Exchange has FTSE; the New York Stock Exchange has DOW and NASDAQ; Euronext Paris has CAC, and the Tokyo Stock Exchange has NIKKEI.

And since we are talking about stock market indexes, here is how they work:

A stock market index will assign all its constituents a weightage to create an average price, and the weighted average of the daily movements in all its constituents reflects the value. Let us create an Index called the DADA-5 based on five companies in the London Stock Exchange with weightage assigned arbitrarily:

Company	Ticker	Industry	Weightage
International Airline Group	IAG	Aviation	15%
British Petroleum	BP.	Oil and Gas	25%
Marks and Spencer	MKS	Retail	20%
Vodafone	VOD	Telecommunication	15%
Royal Bank of Scotland	RBS	Banking	25%

I will pick 02 January 2020 (the first trading day of the year) as the starting point for the index using the actual closing prices on that day for these shares to create the index value on the day:

Ticker	Weightage	Closing Value	Index Value (Weightage x Closing Value
IAG	15%	£ 6.3620	0.9543
BP.	25%	£ 4.8085	1.2021
MKS	20%	£ 2.1410	0.4282
VOD	15%	£ 1.4780	0.2217
RBS	25%	£ 2.4430	0.6108
DADA-5 Index on 02 January 2020			**3.4171**

To show movement, let us take the COVID-19 peak, for example, the closing prices on 15 April 2020.

Ticker	Weightage	Closing Value	Index Value (Weightage x Closing Value
IAG	15%	£ 2.1780	0.3267
BP.	25%	£ 2.9970	0.7493
MKS	20%	£ 0.9916	0.1983
VOD	15%	£ 1.0800	0.1620
RBS	25%	£ 1.0430	0.2608
DADA-5 Index on 15 April 2020			**1.6970**

The tables above show that DADA-5 dropped about 1.72 points or just over 50%, from 3.4171 to 1.6970. That is precisely how stock market indices work, just on a greater scale. They will, to maintain fair representation, change the constituents and weightages from time to time, using what they consider as more representative companies.

I was running an index for all my selected shares when I started off in 1999. I used to call it the DADA-20.

Industries that Focus on Essentials of Life

This is a rule that I base on a simple fact of life as I see it. As human beings, there are things we want, and there are things we need. 'Wants' are discretionary, and we can choose whether to spend on them or not. 'Needs' are requirements that we cannot avoid, and we will spend on them, no matter what.

Needs, in their more extreme form, are Essentials of Life. No matter what happens, people will need a place to live in, food and water, and clothes and medication.

There are other areas like utilities, telecommunication, transportation, banking and media, for example, which have become Essentials of Life (or Needs) just because of our dependency on them. Entertainment options like Netflix could now (after us having spent the best part of the year locked up due to COVID-19) also be classified as 'Needs'.

As there is no definition of what constitutes Essentials of Life, I would encourage you to at least assess each company you consider investing in against this test.

For every company you consider, ask yourself a question: What could prevent people from spending money on the products or services offered by the target company? Then assess the probability of that happening.

Then there are other companies that deal in 'Wants'. People may not always spend on holidays, travel, hospitality, luxury goods and general retail. I describe them as 'Non-Essentials of Life'. Some products qualify as 'Needs' but are 'high-end' and therefore 'Wants'. For example, we all need clothes, but Primark is a Need, while Armani is a Want.

I prefer to invest in 'Needs' rather than 'Wants'. I find them more stable, and if the company has a strong history, I look to buy them when their share price drops due to market sentiment rather than their own individual performance. In such cases, their price tends to bounce back quite well.

The example below shows the impact of the COVID-19 crisis on four companies. I classify two as Needs and two as Wants:

Company	**Needs / Wants**	**Industry**
Severn Trent (SVT)	Needs	Utilities - Gas and Water
GlaxoSmithKline (GSK)	Needs	Pharmaceuticals
Whitbread (WTB)	Wants	Travel and Hospitality
Carnival (CCL)	Wants	Cruise Holidays

The reference dates are 02 January 2020 (before the crisis started), 31 March 2020 (peak of the crisis) and 30 June 2020 (beginning of the first recovery):

Company	02 January 2020	Fluctuation ←← →→	31 March 2020	Fluctuation ←← →→	30 June 2020
SVT	£ 25.15	↓9.34%↓	£ 22.80	↑8.73%↑	£ 24.79
GSK	£ 17.77	↓14.78%↓	£ 15.15	↑8.05%↑	£ 16.37
WTB	£ 42.06	↓38.11%↓	£ 26.03	↓14.64%↓	£ 22.22
CCL	£ 36.48	↓73.11%↓	£ 9.81	↑00.01%↑	£ 9.85

The 'Needs' tend to have more resilience as compared to the 'Wants'. Admittedly, this example is based on selective dates, as there are companies that may have a mix of both and others that will defy the trend. But it demonstrates the rule I follow.

Growth in Revenues, Profits and Dividends for Five Years

While there are quite a few factors to consider when you assess a company's financial health (see ***Learn to Read the Accounts***), the one that matters most to me is the Income Statement, more specifically Revenue and Profitability. And what I look for is a growth trend in both.

If a company can demonstrate growth in both revenues and profit over a five-year stretch, then to me, it is a very good indicator of its sustainability and resilience. That means safety for me as an investor with a reasonable probability of reward. In reality, though, I will settle for stability in revenue and profits if there are patterns of growth in those five years.

The other factor that I feel protects me, combined with the two I mentioned in the previous paragraph, is growth in dividend. If the company is prepared to share its return and has the confidence to increase it year on year, that provides me with a lot of reassurance and incentive to hold.

Take a look at a few examples based on this criterion:

Imperial Brands (IMB)			
Year End	**Revenue**	**Pre-Tax Profit**	**Dividend**
30 September 2015	£ 25,289 M	£ 1,756 M	£ 1.4100
30 September 2016	£ 27,634 M	£ 907 M	£ 1.5520
30 September 2017	£ 30,247 M	£ 1,861 M	£ 1.7070
30 September 2018	£ 30,066 M	£ 1,823 M	£ 1.8780
30 September 2019	£ 31,594 M	£ 1,690 M	£ 2.0660

At the time I wrote this book, this was my favourite company. Even when COVID-19 hit everyone hard, and companies were completely cutting back their dividends, IMB cut its dividend by just a third and retained strong financial performance despite the circumstances. People consider smoking as an Essential of Life for some reason, but that's not for me to judge. I will quietly profit from it.

Legal and General Group (LGEN)			
Year End	**Revenue**	**Pre-Tax Profit**	**Dividend**
31 December 2015	£ 6,321 M	£ 1,414 M	£ 0.1340
31 December 2016	£ 10,252 M	£ 1,517 M	£ 0.1435
31 December 2017	£ 7,932 M	£ 2,061 M	£ 0.1535

31 December 2018	£ 12,843 M	£ 2,129 M	£ 0.1642
31 December 2019	£ 15,203 M	£ 2,156 M	£ 0.1757

LGEN is on my watchlist just because of these statistics. I have not invested in it yet simply because I have never managed to catch the share at a price that would make that dividend high enough yield. I would love to buy it at around £1.70, but it has been averaging well over £2.50.

Vodafone Group (VOD)			
Year End	**Revenue**	**Pre-Tax Profit**	**Dividend**
31 March 2016	€ 49,810 M	(€ 190 M)	€ 0.1448
31 March 2017	€ 47,631 M	€ 2,792 M	€ 0.1477
31 March 2018	€ 46,571 M	€ 3,878 M	€ 0.1507
31 March 2019	€ 43,666 M	(€ 2,613 M)	€ 0.0900
31 March 2020	€ 44,974 M	€ 795 M	€ 0.0900

While I like the industry in which Vodafone operates, their numbers make me uncomfortable. Declining revenues along with two years of losses and a cut in dividends. It is not a company I would ideally look to invest in based on my rules. And if I were to, I would do a lot more research to get comfortable about the variations in revenue and losses.

Mediclinic International (MDC)			
Year End	**Revenue**	**Pre-Tax Profit**	**Dividend**
31 March 2016	£ 2,107 M	£ 245 M	£ 0.0790
31 March 2017	£ 2,749 M	£ 307 M	£ 0.0790
31 March 2018	£ 2,876 M	(£ 479 M)	£ 0.0790

31 March 2019	£ 2,932 M	(£ 137 M)	£ 0.0790
31 March 2020	£ 3,083 M	(£ 275 M)	£ 0.0320

I like the business model, as it is a global healthcare service provider, and if they can maintain quality, there is no shortage of business. But while their revenues have grown year on year, their losses in the last three years put me off, and they do not have confidence in their dividend. The dividend was not growing even when they were profitable, and now they have reduced it further due to their losses. It looks unusual and does not come across as instantly appealing. I would not buy into it, no matter what the reasons behind those numbers.

Growing or Stable Cash Flows, and Stable or Declining Borrowings

There are several balance sheet elements to consider. The classic investors' ratios are Earning Per Share (EPS) and the Price-Earnings Ratio (PE Ratio).

EPS is calculated (in its simplest form) as:

$$\frac{\textbf{Net Profit – Preferred Divided}}{\textbf{Weighted Average Common Shares}}$$

The higher the EPS, the better the share.

PE Ratio is calculated as:

$$\frac{\textbf{Share Price}}{\textbf{EPS}}$$

The lower the PE Ratio, the better the investment is likely to be.

Beyond these very standard ratios, I prefer to look at two balance sheet aspects to judge the company's financial health.

I look for liquidity, shown by cash or bank balances. I prefer to see that number increasing or stable over five years. That shows to me the company is generating enough cash and can sustain itself. It is not over-investing to get an increase in its revenues (which is what was discussed earlier in the book).

I also look for borrowings (current or non-current). This is to make sure that the liquidity is not increasing because of an increase in borrowing. I prefer to see borrowings stable or declining.

As I am looking for high-dividend yields in my strategy, these elements, along with the revenue, profit and dividend information, form a key part of my buying strategy. I do not really rely as much on the ratios I explained, though I tend to rely more on the rest of this information when deciding what to buy. But the ratios are useful indicators.

A Dividend Yield of 10%

Companies do not give you a 10% dividend yield intentionally. You, as an investor, have to find that moment in time when you can buy a share that will, because of the price you were able to buy it at, result in a return of a 10% yield.

The 10% target has become a fundamental part of my buying strategy. When I switched to being more focused on shares that gave dividends, I was looking for 5% so that in case I was unable to sell it off, I at least had some recurring return to fall back on. And I started discovering that there were companies out there where I could get a dividend higher than 10% if I bought them at the right time, as then I would not have to worry about selling at all.

The approach here is to identify a company that:
a) Is profitable and issues a regular dividend.
b) The share price versus dividend gives a relatively high yield.
c) Identify a share price at which the dividend yield would become 10%.
d) Wait for it to come to you and buy when it gets there.

I stalked British Petroleum (BP.) for over a month when I saw its share price was close to around 7.5% to 8% of its annual dividend. BP's annual dividend for 2019 was €0.4125 (£0.3750) per share.

When I began tracking it around mid-May 2020, it was priced at around £3.40 (so over 10%). Given the risk of a cut in dividend due to COVID-19, I decided to go for a target price of £3.05, which would give me a dividend yield of 12.5%. Took me a month of waiting and seeing the price shoot up to £3.65 before it finally dropped to £3.05 in early July 2020, and I bought it.

The moral of the story is that you have to create your own 10% yield by identifying potential shares and hunting them down patiently till they come to your price. It is very frustrating and demands a lot of patience (especially when you miss them by a few pence).

However, it is very important to remember this. *You are only in control of your destiny when you are buying. When you have bought, you are no longer in charge*. The effort and patience you put in when you bought it will then count. See ***You Make Money When You Buy*** for more details on this topic.

Buy Low and Sell High – Over 52 Weeks

The heading, of course, states the obvious. But what does a high and low price even mean? My tracking range is usually 52 weeks, as, beyond that, I feel data become less relevant for decision making. In some cases, I would even consider limiting the range to 26 weeks or 13 weeks, but the 52 weeks range is more conventional.

Once you have identified the right share, you need to make sure it is priced right. *There is no good share or bad share in my view. A very good company may be a bad investment to buy if it is overpriced, while a really poor company may present a great investment opportunity to buy if it is priced too low.*

I do not like buying airline stocks as I do not believe it is a good business to invest in. But I have still bought EasyJet twice and IAG once, and those trades gave me fabulous returns. IAG resulted in a 23% gain in one trading day. That was because these trades in companies, that I typically consider as unsuitable in line with my strategy, were based on a price that was very low given the circumstances.

Assess your portfolio of companies that meet the rules you deem appropriate—I have defined mine in this chapter. Then, work out the right price you would pay for each of them and base it close to the lower end of the 52-week range. Then just wait for it to come to you.

Low Price Based on Market Conditions rather than Problems with the Company

When I see markets collapse and jump based on news or rumours, I am convinced that most part-time traders are buying and selling based on sentiment, unsubstantiated advice or pure emotion. Frankly, I am not sure if most even know what they are doing. Some of the buying tactics people have discussed with me are horrendous.

Not every bit of global news has a detrimental impact on each and every company out there. On the contrary, some companies may thrive, but the market reacts differently.

When Brexit was announced, almost every company dropped in value for a while, as they did during COVID-19. The question to ask is, were both these events equally bad for all companies? Or were people just selling because that is what they do when they hear bad news?

The best time to invest in a company is when the market falls in unison, as that usually has nothing to do with a company with a strong financial and performance history. Assess the news causing the market to drop, and see if it has any impact on the company you are interested in. If not, then apply all other rules and do not let the opportunity go to waste.

To quote Winston Churchill:

"Never let a good crisis go to waste".

The chart below shows a pattern of such crises when all seemed lost and people sold in droves:

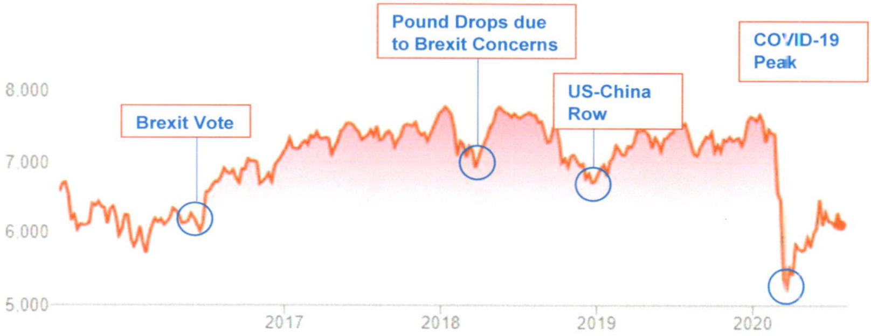

The chart shows four crashes with reasons. I see four opportunities. Brexit, the US-China row or COVID-19 were not bad for every company out there. Some would have even benefited from it. So, when everyone rushes to sell like a herd of sheep, it presents an incredible opportunity to purchase a good company at the right price. It might represent an opportunity that you wait for, but it never usually comes. And as the chart shows, it all tends to bounce back. Just make sure you have the ability to hold on to the investment for a while.

The one critical pitfall of a drop in share price which you must look out for is when a company with a perfectly reasonable history drops its price without any impending global crisis. That is when it may tick off all the above rules, yet it might have an underlying, more sinister problem. If you see a share price drop without a global reason, that is a massive red flag.

My example is Petrofac. It was my 'go-to' share for making trading gains during 2015 and 2016. It had a great financial history and would fluctuate nicely, presenting a series of opportunities to buy low and sell high. But I missed the underlying cause of these fluctuations. The Executive Management was under investigation by the Serious Fraud Office for bribery. It led to executives being terminated, and the share price dived finally without recovery, and I was left holding quite a bit of it in 2017. It is one of the 9 times I have lost money on the stock market, and it was the most significant loss of them all. It was also the last time I lost money trading.

Petrofac changed my strategy to move to long-term investment rather than buying with the sole intention of a capital gain. I lost money, but I learnt from it. Petrofac was the pain that inspired me to come up with the idea of defining an Ideal Investment.

Key Points from this Chapter

- ✓ Focus on companies that are constituents of a Primary Index.

- ✓ Invest in 'Needs' and not 'Wants'. Companies that produce goods or services that classify as Essentials of Life or 'Needs' tend to be more sustainable and are more resilient to crises than companies that operate in discretionary products, or 'Wants'.

- ✓ Go for companies with growing or stable revenue in the past five years. That demonstrates the company has demand and is resilient.

- ✓ The above rule should be backed by growing or stable profits for the past five years. Without profits, a company is not really a business.

- ✓ While revenue and profits are good for the business, you only benefit if they share them with you. Buy companies with growing or stable dividend for the past five years. It shows the company has confidence in its own ability to generate liquidity. And from an investors' perspective, you can hold while frequently benefiting without selling.

- ✓ The balance sheet of your target companies should ideally show growing or stable cash flows and stable or declining borrowings (Current and Non-Current). The ability to generate cash without reliance on borrowings is a very good indicator of the financial health of the company.

- ✓ Target dividend yield at 10% of current market price, as that is what it will cost you to buy those shares. Buy at the right price to make sure that your market price yields a high dividend. Define the right price and wait for the company's share price to come to your price.

- ✓ The ideal buying price should be a market price close to a share's 52 Week Low price. That will allow you to buy a good company at a lower price.

- ✓ The market price should be low due to overall market conditions rather than issues with the company itself. Good companies bounce back as the price drop just reflects investor sentiment and herd mentality. But watch out for shares that drop in price during stable market conditions. That is a red flag, and the company in question may have underlying issues that need to be understood.

A Market you do not Control

"I compare investing in a stock market to riding a wave. You can never control what it will do. You need to know what you can handle, when you can get in and when to jump off. Just wait for the right wave."

I dare not try to predict what the stock market will do, at least not beyond the current day. It reacts to just about anything in the world and usually reacts in its entirety. It reacts to economic updates, to political events worldwide, to pandemics, to rumours and statements, and to wars. A positive vibe can drive the most share prices up, even if it does not apply to all shares, and negative sentiment can bring it all down.

It does not always behave in a logical manner, and it tends to reflect people's emotive reactions to breaking news and events. You could also believe in conspiracy theories that there are times where the markets may also be responding to news intentionally created to trigger a stock market response to benefit the powers-that-be. Not that I am at all suggesting that ever happens!

The point I am trying to make is that it will react to things that you cannot always forecast and react in ways you cannot comprehend. So recognising and accepting that from the onset is important: you are in a world you do not control. To pretend to have any sort of control can have quite devastating consequences. It is an uncertain place to be, and you have to accept that and learn to deal with it. The worst thing you can do in uncertainty is to incorrectly follow a path of a false certainty.

The chart below shows daily trends of the FTSE-100 during 2020, from 01 July 2020 to 30 September 2020 – probably one of the most uncertain and volatile eras of our lifetimes when the world was rife with COVID-19 news, a global recession and the controversy-laden build-up to the US elections:

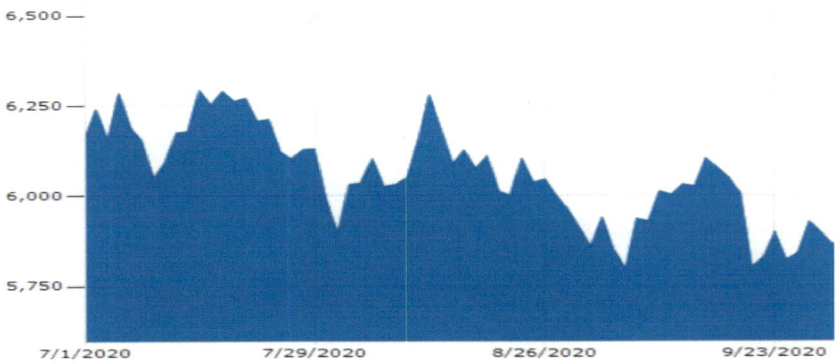

www.markets.businessinsider.com

As the chart above shows, there were numerous opportunities where the markets dived heavily and then jumped back up quickly, all in response to the spate of news coming in which were either negative or positive, and even contradictory. But the narrative was essentially the same: COVID-19 was spreading; there were global lockdowns to manage it; several vaccines were being developed; the economy was in a terrible shape, and there was a close battle in US elections between Donald Trump and Joe Biden.

However, the market kept reacting as if there was a surprise every day because the news headlines made it seem that way. This is simply people reacting to the news, and they create the waves that an emotionless buyer must learn to ride.

What you are looking for in this uncertainty and volatility are companies that are perfectly good businesses, but their share prices are being impacted by the herd mentality that seemingly drives the volatility in stock market prices. I do not think a lot of people simply buy and sell for a good enough reason. And that creates the sort of opportunity I spend days waiting for: a growing, profitable company that has seen its share price suddenly drop, resulting in its existing dividend yield becoming very high. These might be companies that perhaps were always highly-priced in the past (for good reason) but now have become very good deals.

While the market is impacted by general sentiment and emotive reactions, it takes down good and bad companies with it and then takes them back up. The trick is to back your game plan and apply it when the conditions are ripe for it to work well.

What you want to look out for are shares within companies that you consider as your ideal investment that have now moved down (to your target buying price) purely due to a general market reaction. You may want to avoid a company where the share price has dropped due to news specific to that company. That is a potential buying hazard, and any such 'opportunity' should be explored and analysed further before you respond to it. The one such hazardous example I have covered in this book is my adventure with Petrofac (PFC) —see ***My Ideal Investment***.

My go-to share for this year was Imperial Brands (IMB), which I have spoken about so fondly in this book. I consider it a robust and stable business as I do not believe people will be giving up tobacco anytime soon. It is stable and profitable, and despite the COVID-19 impact, it retained its profitability and paid out two-thirds of its already high dividend yield. Nothing that happened this year should have really impacted its price significantly, yet here is how it reacted to the market for the same period I have shown above:

www.youinvest.co.uk

IMB has followed a slightly similar pattern to the FTSE-100, where it dived and rose with the market, while ultimately its results showed almost no impact on business. But the price was impacted purely by market sentiment. Therefore, I kept buying at every opportunity to add to my existing holding. To me, it was a fabulous opportunity to top on an investment that still yields more than 10% in dividend alone.

At this point in my book, I want to like to pause and take this opportunity to say a massive thank you to the thousands of 'herd mentality' investors of this world for creating these waves of opportunity for me! Please continue to exist and keep creating these opportunities for me. I will always remain grateful.

Back to the book—I would like to compare the IMB situation to another share that reflects the opposite end of the spectrum and one I dare not touch: Carnival (CCL).

Carnival is one of the largest leisure cruise travel groups globally and, based on the last few years' financial performance, one of the most successful ones. I never invested in it because it does not qualify under my 'Needs' category as it is essentially a 'Want'. And that risk approach was highlighted brutally when COVID-19 struck, and there were horror stories of passengers stuck on virus-infected cruise ships. With all but essential travel suspended long-term, I cannot imagine being involved or associated with a business worse than leisure cruise holidays.

CCL shares dropped quite heavily, as you would logically expect, but I regularly saw CCL share movements in either the top five risers or the top five fallers every week far too regularly. It would seemingly react sharply to every bit of good and bad news, while in the long-term, the news was consistently bad: that all international leisure travel will remain suspended for very a long time.

There was no concrete indicator for cruise holidays resuming any time soon.

When you look at CCL versus FTSE-100, like we did for IMB, it presents a picture that I cannot logically understand. But that is what happened – a series of jumps and dives:

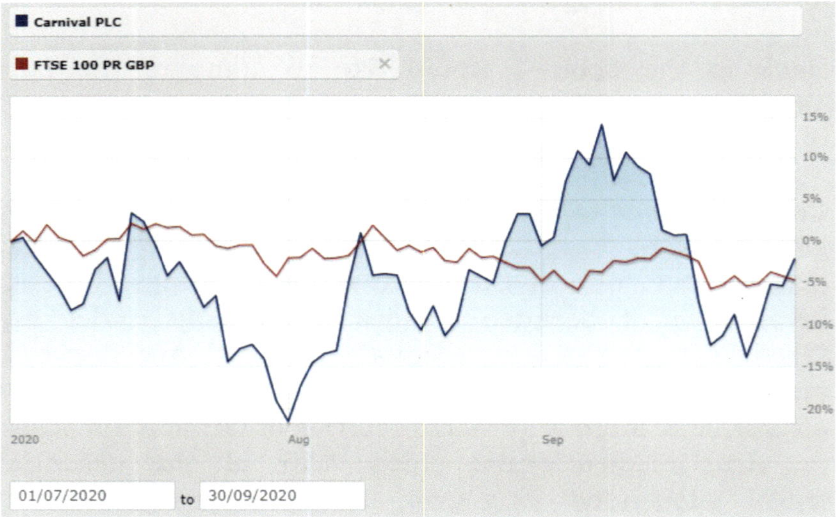

www.youinvest.co.uk

After years of success, CCL predictably reported abysmal results. Their revenue collapsed, and they reported a huge loss, and there were no surprises there because of the way the world was at the time. Yet the price, after an initial collapse, kept jagging sharply up and down without any concrete news of recovery in the business. Look at August and look at September.

There was no logical reason for that movement, and yet it happened. I simply cannot work out how and why that would happen if I analyse it with a rational mindset because the outlook is just negative on a long-term basis.

To me, that is the uncontrollable aspect of the stock market that I must accept and learnt to deal with if I have to survive this market. Clearly, there is money to be made in these movements, but CCL as an industry is outside of my risk appetite level, so I stayed away. I cannot work out a rock bottom price for this business nor convince myself that it has the future demand to survive. It does not fit my strategy. There are others out there who may understand this better, but since I don't, I will not touch it.

I did, however, opt to go against my risk-averse strategy and benefit from such spikes in International Airline Group (IAG) earlier in the year. I wouldn't ever invest in airlines long-term, but this time it was too good to miss. And while it does not fit my ideal investment profile, I do understand that business quite well and was able to predict a safe rock-bottom price, then rely on the upcoming emotive optimism of the herd investors. I have discussed that trade in detail in the chapter, ***You Make Money When You Buy***.

Market volatility is your best friend and your worst enemy, which depends on your ability to identify and understand the right companies to buy and their right buying price. It gets exceedingly dull when the market is stable or one-directional as there is no clear opportunity. The game is only really on when it spikes in both directions, and in that regard, 2020 was a year littered with opportunity.

As I discussed before, you do not have to predict the market, and you shouldn't even try to. You just need to know what to buy and at what price to buy it. Once you have that, just sit back and wait for the right wave to take your preferred share to your price.

I have set up buy trades for days on end, waiting for the right 'wave' to knock the share price down to my level only to see it miss repeatedly. I would then do the same thing again and again until it either finally hit the buy price or rises out of my buying range.

With this strategy, all you then have to do is ride the wave wherever it takes you. If you have the right share at the right price, then enjoy the ride and know when to jump off!

Key Points from this Chapter

- ✓ A stock market is largely unpredictable as a whole, and it reacts to people's emotional perception of news. And it drags good and bad companies upwards or downwards without a good enough reason specific to those companies. That is what creates opportunity.

- ✓ Do not try to predict the stock market and accept its uncertainty. Focus on identifying companies that fit your investment preference and their ideal price. Then wait for the unpredictable market to create waves that allow you to buy at the price you deem appropriate and ultimately sell at the price you want.

- ✓ In general, I do not believe people buy or sell for a good enough reason, and there is a herd mentality that impacts the market and ultimately share prices. Learn to identify good companies that drop value just because the stock market is dropping for a completely unrelated reason and buy in at your preferred price. Refer to my IMB example during COVID-19.

Investments are Emotionless

"You invest based on numbers and cold hard facts, not based on what you may like or dislike. That is emotional interference, and there is no room for that in business."

I detest smoking, and there is no other way I can describe it. I cannot understand why people would cause themselves and others around them such incredible self-harm. I truly believe it is an absolutely terrible industry. It somehow manages to avoid regulations and market itself to the most vulnerable and impressionable among us – usually teenagers – to create customers for life. It has created an image in our minds over time that it is somehow cool to smoke and to be seen smoking. There are cultures where a person is only considered mature when they start to smoke. Somehow all this is a legally permissible business, and there is a big market for it.

I have never smoked in my life. When I was very young, my father warned me that he would kick me out of the house if he ever caught me smoking. It was valuable advice as I resisted taking up smoking throughout my life, even in my most impressionable years. I have used the same quote on my children, and it seems to have worked (at least I think so!).

On the contrary, I absolutely adore commercial aviation. If I had the eyesight for it, I would have been a commercial pilot without hesitation. This limitation never impacted my passion, and I have avidly studied aviation and commercial aircraft and found ways to manoeuvre my accounting and audit career to allow me to work with ten different airlines. It is the most incredible industry to be in, and I cannot think of a more fascinating and exciting business to be a part of.

But when it comes to investment, I have found my greatest success in tobacco, and I would not ever invest long-term in an airline. And I invest that way because that is the path defined by numbers and facts, not by my personal likes and dislikes. There is no room for personal preference in business.

When I began investing, I stayed away from tobacco-associated industries. After all, I detested smoking and had ethical and moral issues in investing in the industry. I would not touch defence stocks either—they cause all the wars out there after all, don't they! But as my approach evolved, I decided to put my personal ethical values aside and make decisions based on numbers and facts.

These companies exist, and they do business that is legal and successful. Whether I buy into them or not, the shares will continue to trade. It is a competitive market, and I eventually decided to go for it. And Imperial Brands (IMB) quickly became a favourite investment. I have explained earlier that this company comes as close as possible to the definition of my perfect investment, as described in the chapter ***My Ideal Investment***.

As it turned out, the switch to IMB worked massively well during 2020 as the company successfully endured the COVID-19 crisis with the most minimal impact. Smoking proved to be a bona fide 'Need' for a lot of people, even during a time when a disease was destroying lungs. Who am I to judge!

Airlines, on the other hand, are terrible businesses. They are an industry that is impacted by external risks that they have no control of. A volcano could go off in the middle of nowhere; a war could break out somewhere, or a couple of countries could disagree on a topic and close borders. This is nothing to do with the airline, but that suddenly means destinations get closed and expensive aircraft cannot be utilised.

Safety comes with a price, and airlines spend a lot to ensure that. They are weak suppliers (with capacity or supply being far greater than demand), resulting in low fares for most of the year just to create demand. And unlike most businesses where the customer is dominant, airlines are also weak customers dealing with almost monopolistic aircraft and engine manufacturers and dominant airports that charge as they please for the right to operate there.

They are also an easy target for regulators, who quite unfairly target them with excessive charges and portray them as being primarily responsible for climate change, despite the industry being responsible for only 2% of all global carbon emissions. Even when all goes perfectly well, a good airline with its massive investment can expect a 5% to 7% return on investment. I can make 10% a year without even trying very hard at the stock market.

Sadly, airlines also qualify as 'Wants'. They have grown their capacity by such excessive volumes that they now almost completely target discretionary spend and are forced to sell at low fares to fill their seats. That is not where I want to invest my hard-earned money.

As I mentioned earlier, commercial aviation is fascinating, and it is an industry that I am passionate about. But I also know it too well. And cold hard facts tell me that it is an industry I should not invest a penny in. The only reason why I ever look to invest in airlines now is that I back my knowledge of the industry and how the prices might rise or fall based on developments and market perception. It is the only deviation I allow myself from my conventional approach of buying long-term in good businesses. And I deviate from it with great caution.

In all my investment strategies and tactics from the day I started, numbers have been the key. Even when my approach was based on pure trend analysis, I was still looking at numbers. As I evolved to targeting capital gains, I still looked at trends but added financial statements. And in my current approach, I have just increased my focus on looking at more numbers. Never have I selected a share based on preference for a company.

I have in the past excluded companies because of ethical reasons (a moral limitation I have now largely overcome), but I have never, ever bought a share because I liked what the company did.

Even when I develop my database of shares to monitor, it is based on where the industry meets the 'Needs' vs 'Wants' test, its revenue, profitability, dividend, debt-equity, and liquidity. I will read recent news on developments and broker advice for reference. But I never buy anything based on whether I like a particular business type.

Never buy on emotion or general advice. Listen to everyone but do your own research and know what you are looking for. Never get too attached to a company, and do not go chasing it if the price is not quite right. Let the share price of the company you have selected, based on the research you have done, drop down to your level.

The only emotion I want you to feel is the only one I allow myself, and that is the pure thrill of victory when you beat the market and make a gain from an investment based on an idea that was purely yours!

Key Points from this Chapter

- ✓ You never invest in companies or businesses that you like. You invest in companies that make business sense based on facts and numbers.

- ✓ I use an Airlines vs Tobacco analogy to describe this. Airlines are truly fascinating for me as an industry. I love nothing more. On the other hand, I detest the Tobacco industry and have never smoked. But Airlines are a terrible business, and the Tobacco industry is very resilient and profitable. I invest in Tobacco and rarely go near Airlines.

- ✓ Select investment based on the following 'non-emotional' criteria:
    - Industries that produce goods or services that are 'Needs' and not 'Wants'.
    - Financial performance with regard to revenue, profitability, dividend, debt-equity, and liquidity is stable or improving.
    - There are no negative or threatening developments specifically for that company in the recent news.
    - ......and not much else!

Cutting your Losses

"I have nothing clever to say about this as this is a lesson I have yet to learn. This chapter is a lecture from me to myself to learn and change my ways."

I have stated at the beginning of this book that my trading record at the time this book was published stood at 76 wins and 9 losses, and that since 2017, I have made 15 profitable trades and 0 losses. That record does give me decent credibility to claim that I have a successful approach to investment, and I certainly have enough confidence in it to thrash out a book about it and explain it with certainty that it will help the reader. But there is one flaw that I have not been able to overcome. I hate selling for a loss!

The general rule of thumb that other traders have used, or at least explained to me, is that they apply a 'Stop Loss' approach to their trades. A Stop Loss simply means that you define a share price level beyond which you are not prepared to allow your share to drop. Beyond that point, you are prepared to sell, accept that loss and exit. That means you live to fight another day. Some people will set that at 5% of their purchase price or 10%, or whatever level defines their risk appetite.

I have held shares that have gone beyond 20% of their purchase price, and they have still bounced back and given me a profit. And this particularly worked well when I changed my investment approach to buying companies that meet my required definition of ***an Ideal Investment***.

This 'bounce-back' ability of good shares puts me off selling them for a loss.

But then I have made 9 losses, some quite large ones. One was where I had a share that became zero value because I just kept holding on to it, having had the opportunity to sell for a loss and recoup something out of it.

I am going to try and create scenarios where I would think that perhaps in those cases, selling for a loss is justifiable. This will be based on my current philosophy and approach to investment rather than any other aspect or experience.

For example, margin traders simply have to sell for a loss if the gap between what they owe the broker develops due to share price erosion, and the gap becomes greater than their deposit. Or scenarios where investments are done using time-limited surplus funds and shares and must be sold by a certain time, as cash is required elsewhere. Since I do not endorse such tactics to investment in the first place, my loss scenarios will not cover that.

Instead, I will cover the following, which are in line with my recommended approach:

Consolidated Investment Gain Higher than Individual Trade Loss

When you identify a quality share, you may want to increase your holding in it over time and at various prices. Your ultimate holding will reflect a net share price that you purchased at. For example:

Transaction Number	Price	Number of Shares	Purchase Value
1	£13	1,000	£13,000
2	£12	2,000	£24,000
3	£11	3,000	£33,000
4	£10	4,000	£40,000
Average Price	**£11**	**10,000**	**£110,000**

If I were to sell these shares for my approximate target margin of 10%, let's say £12, I would get £120,000 and make an overall profit of £10,000 on a £110,000 investment. Not a bad achievement, in my view.

However, in line with how I track and report performance, this 'successful trade' would look like:

Transaction Number	Number of Shares	Buying Price	Selling Price	Gain / (Loss)
1	1,000	£13	£12	(£1,000)
2	2,000	£12	£12	£0
3	3,000	£11	£12	£3,000
4	4,000	£10	£12	£8,000
Overall Gain				**£10,000**

I would report this as two profitable transactions, one breakeven transaction and one loss-making transaction. Should I, in this case, be happy because I met my overall 10% gain target or hold till all my individual purchases are profitable?

Logically, if I achieved my overall objective of the investment and made around 10%, I should sell. But I have been stubborn and held on to shares because I hate the idea of any transaction making a loss. This is the first lesson I would like to learn and implement.

A Better Opportunity to Invest

There may be a time where you are holding on to an investment, which is currently at a loss but not to a point where it is alarming. However, a surprise new opportunity shows up, which looks better in all respects to the one you currently hold.

You can either approach the new investment with additional surplus funds, or you may want to make a call on whether it is worth selling the investment in hand.

This is something that I have actually done once where I cleared out a lot of old shares that had developed a long-term loss in August 2019 and used proceeds from those loss-making sales to fund the opportunity to invest in tobacco through Imperial Brands (IMB). However, these share prices had eroded significantly and over a long time, and I could have sold them for a lower loss earlier. It should have never got to this point—another lesson to learn.

Companies Where Business Case No Longer Applies

When you invest in a company with a particular business case (in my case, usually a high dividend yield with a prospect of a 10% capital gain) and things change, you may want to reconsider it. The likelihood of recovery over a reasonable amount of time may change as the scenario you had assessed at the time of investment has changed. At that point, you might consider selling with a loss. If you have waited an adequate time, and the share price has fallen, and the news feed isn't optimistic about recovery, it might be time to walk away before it gets worse.

I made this mistake with Petrofac (PFC). I have made quite a few successful trades, and at the time, my game plan was not based on dividend. The share price dived after the company came under investigation for bribery, and the CEO was interrogated by the police.

At that point, PFC became a share I would not have bought had I been looking to buy. However, I kept holding on to it in the hope of recovery. It never happened, and I sold for a bigger loss than I would have made had I realised earlier that it was over.

This is probably the main lesson for me to learn. I changed my investment model based on this outcome, and nothing I have purchased since has faced such a risk. But I have to be more aware of when to leave rather than hold out on a wing and a prayer!

I still do not recommend a fixed Stop Loss rule of selling shares if they go below a certain percentage below the purchase price because every investment should be assessed differently. There may be shares that have simply dropped because the market reacted as a whole in response to a global event (for example, Brexit or just about any US election). If nothing has changed in the company I have invested in, and the reaction is just to the market due to a particular event, I still would not sell.

Also, view shares that give out good dividends differently, as you have bought for those with a long-term, 'hold-for-life' view. Just assess them to see if they are still operating as you expected them to and hold on to them, regardless of how the market impacts their share price. Their market price changes should be allowed a lot more flexibility.

Key Points from this Chapter

✓ Unlike other chapters, in this one, I am not preaching about what I practise, but about something that I have to learn and improve myself.

✓ There will be circumstances when it makes more sense to sell shares for a loss rather than hold on to them.

✓ Your consolidated investment into a company, comprising multiple trades, may be profitable. But you may be showing a loss on individual trades. Sell based on consolidated cost rather than individual trade cost if the overall results meet your business case target.

✓ You may find a situation where selling shares for a loss allows you to free up surplus funds to move to a potentially more profitable trade or another investment opportunity.

✓ You may hold shares in a company, where the circumstances of the company change irreversibly, resulting in a drop in share price. In that case, you have to assess whether you would have invested based on the new circumstances the company faces. If not, then consider taking a loss and getting out before the price gets worse. Revise your business case.

✓ Do not have a one-size-fits-all approach like a percentage based 'Stop Loss' for all investments. Assess each investment as a unique situation and then decide on the best path forward.

- ✓ If the share price is simply a reaction to a change in the entire stock market, do not be overly concerned. Good companies which are resilient to market condition bounce back, especially if your intention is to hold the share on a long-term basis for dividend. Just make sure there is no company-specific negative news.

Conclusion

I am not a stock market expert, and I do not claim to be one. I have not written this book for financial markets, professionals or people who spend their workdays researching companies applying far more creative and lucrative tactics to investments in the stock market. This book is not meant to be for anyone like that.

But I am someone who has learnt to make money off the stock market consistently and safely over a very long time. In that time, I have developed and evolved tactics that can be understood with ease and applied with relative safety and for a reasonable gain. That is where I confidently claim my success and credibility.

I intended to compile in this book the entirety of my experience in the stock market, and every possible tactic I have used in my trading life, and how I have evolved the approach. And while maintaining my stance that I am not a stock market expert, I do claim to have a successful and trading record (See ***My Trading History*** at the end of the book). I have managed to sustain that through tricky trading periods such as the 2008 financial crisis, Brexit vote in 2016 and the COVID-19 Pandemic. So the approach, while simple and with its limitations, definitely works, and that is what I have tried to demonstrate.

The book covers my experience from 1999, the different investment models I have applied, along with their pros and cons. I have explained the logic of each strategy and the reason for evolution to the next one, along with the results.

I have covered the basics of how to get started, how to develop your own investment model, and then what sort of investments to target. In effect, I believe I have created a reference book to develop a simple, profitable working model for a part-time investor. I wish I knew all this when I started out; the journey would have been more enjoyable.

The other thing that I really wanted to pass across to any reader is the thrill that I feel when I take on the markets and win. The stock market is inherently designed to disadvantage the part-time, individual investor. It is too tempting in its lure for a casual trader to succeed consistently if they approach it incorrectly, And that plays perfectly in favour of the more informed, institutional investor with greater knowledge and insight.

We, the part-timers, are supposed to lose so the bigger players can win. That is how I like to think of it. To go and succeed in that environment as the underdog feels brilliant. I tell myself that every time I make a profit, I beat the odds, and I out-thought someone far more resourceful and clever than me. Every investment is Rocky Balboa vs Apollo Creed… and you want the result from the sequel!

There are safer ways to succeed in the stock market. You can invest in mutual funds or buy Exchange Traded Funds and let someone else manage your funds for you for a safe and consistent reasonable return. But what is the thrill in that? You are not the master of your own fate, and the success is not yours to claim. Perhaps I am a control freak, and so I cannot even think of letting someone else manage my funds. But more than anything,

I want to be the one that beats the market with my ideas. And with time and experience, I have learnt to back myself with confidence.

Though the odds are stacked against you, the stock market represents an equal opportunity for all to either make it work to your advantage or to lose out. While this statement is paradoxical, it is the situation you face the moment you decide to enter the market. The market fluctuates for you as it does for all to see, and the data to make the call when to buy or sell is available to all. It is your choice about what data you look at, how you interpret it and then the plan you make based on that before pressing the button to buy.

The stock market was probably not designed for the way it is being used right now. Investment is not betting on a share price to rise based on pure speculation and then selling it for a gain. Investment means committing to a business on a long-term basis because you believe in its sustainable success and intend to gain from that. But, the reality is what it is, and people make money from all means of activities on the stock market.

However, the very essence of the stock market remains valid. If you stop playing the stock market and use it for what it was meant for, which is to be a platform to allow investment in publicly listed companies, you increase your chance of success. Because when you do that, you are no longer playing the stock market or speculating on gains and losses caused by turbulence and volatility. You are simply buying a share of ownership in a business that you believe is successful and want to benefit from its profits. When you do that, you are no longer investing in the stock market but in a good business. That is ultimately where I have found sustained success.

Select good businesses that produce goods or services that are essentials of life or 'Needs' and be a lot more careful before you invest in companies that produce goods or services that requires discretionary income or 'Wants'.

The final and perhaps most important objective of this book is to give you a tried and tested strategy for a safe but profitable start. The stock market can be a confusing place when you enter. I have explained how to fund your investments, how to select what to buy, when to buy it and when you hold and / or exit.

This is all tried and tested over a significant duration and across multiple global spikes caused by crises and bursts of optimism. I would not have published all this if I had not acquired an adequate level of confidence in what I do. This approach has seen me ride the stock market out safely and profitably. I want you to at least consider this as your starting point while you learn. And then evolve your strategy further with experience. Do not rush into it thinking you can conquer the market from Day 1. That is how people get wiped out by it. It is the story of every failed stock market investor, or the ones, at least, that I have ever come across.

This was the story I heard from people who tried to deter me from ever starting out. I started despite being told repeatedly that I would not be able to make any money on the stock market. Yet here I am encouraging you to start, but in a manner where you minimise your risk.

It ultimately is for you to decide the investment model you follow, and I hope I have given you the information required for you to develop or modify your own approach that gives you an advantage in this business. Start slow and base it (initially at least) on the approach I have defined to learn how the stock market works. And then, with time, you will develop your own model that will stand the test of time.

No matter what you do, do not rely on blind luck. Every move you make should have a business case defining when to get in, a reason to hold and when to get out. You will still need a bit of luck but reduce your reliance on it by applying the tactics explained in this book.

I hope I have guided you and inspired you with my words. Now go out there and enjoy the thrill of the chase and the joy of winning!

My Trading History

London Stock Exchange 2008 to 2012

Purchase Date	Sale / Dividend Date	Share	Buying Price / Share	Selling Price / Share	Dividend / Share	Gain / (Loss)	Return on Investment
01 December 2008	22 December 2008	LMI	£7.75	£8.51	--	£0.76	170.49%
05 December 2008	11 December 2008	PFD	£0.18	£0.25	--	£0.07	2333.33%
16 December 2008	06 January 2009	ORE	£0.07	£0.08	--	£0.01	301.79%
19 December 2008	12 January 2009	MEC	£0.01	£0.02	--	£0.01	1283.42%
13 January 2009	17 September 2009	REX	£3.19	£2.73	--	-£0.47	-21.63%
14 January 2009	02 March 2010	ARI	£4.97	£5.35	--	£0.38	6.78%
23 January 2009	07 September 2009	GEMD	£2.49	£2.75	--	£0.27	17.20%
	05 May 2009	ARI	--	--	£0.18	£0.18	
22 May 2009	15 September 2009	PVCS	£0.83	£0.84	--	£0.01	4.58%
	02 July 2009	REX	--	--	£0.12	£0.12	
08 July 2009	15 September 2009	PVCS	£0.75	£0.84	--	£0.09	63.05%
27 July 2009	17 September 2009	REX	£2.85	£2.73	--	-£0.12	-30.59%
19 August 2009	17 September 2009	REX	£1.50	£2.73	--	£1.23	1027.91%
26 August 2009	15 September 2009	PVCS	£0.78	£0.84	--	£0.06	138.19%
15 September 2009	17 September 2009	REX	£2.60	£2.73	--	£0.12	849.77%
21 September 2009	08 October 2009	REX	£2.63	£2.76	--	£0.13	103.37%
	02 October 2009	ARI	--	--	£0.06	£0.06	
26 October 2009	02 August 2019	PFD	£0.38	£0.37	--	-£0.01	-0.25%
27 October 2009	02 August 2019	PVCS	£0.72	£0.25	--	-£0.46	-6.63%
12 March 2010	10 May 2010	SKS	£1.02	£1.16	--	£0.14	84.15%
05 June 2010	02 August 2019	PFD	£0.25	£0.37	--	£0.12	5.29%
	06 September 2010	PVCS	--	--	£0.02	£0.02	
	08 June 2010	SKS	--	--	£0.02	£0.02	
10 October 2010	03 April 2014	YELL	£0.15	Written Off	--	-£0.15	-100.00%
	20 October 2010	PVCS	--	--	£0.01	£0.01	

London Stock Exchange 2008 to 2012 (Continued)

Purchase Date	Sale / Dividend Date	Share	Buying Price / Share	Selling Price / Share	Dividend / Share	Gain / (Loss)	Return on Investment
16 March 2011	16 May 2011	DXNS	£0.16	£0.18	--	£0.02	90.11%
25 March 2011	31 October 2013	CWC	£0.43	£0.47	--	£0.03	2.74%
	06 August 2011	PVCS	--	--	£0.02	£0.02	
	08 December 2011	CWC	--	--	£0.03	£0.03	
19 August 2011	14 October 2011	BP.	£3.94	£4.15	--	£0.21	34.33%
	20 January 2012	CWC	--	--	£0.02	£0.02	
18 January 2012	17 August 2012	TSCO	£3.20	£3.41	--	£0.22	11.62%
	07 July 2012	TSCO	--	--	£0.10	£0.10	
	13 August 2012	CWC	--	--	£0.03	£0.03	
26 September 2012	09 November 2012	SKS	£0.78	£0.85	--	£0.07	77.26%
23 November 2012	01 September 2013	VOD	£1.57	£1.65	--	£0.07	5.91%

London Stock Exchange 2013 to 2017

Purchase Date	Sale / Dividend Date	Share	Buying Price / Share	Selling Price / Share	Dividend / Share	Gain / (Loss)	Return on Investment
	11 January 2013	CWC	--	--	£0.01	£0.01	
03 April 2013	24 April 2013	DEB	£0.84	£0.86	--	£0.02	45.98%
14 June 2013	31 July 2013	FGP	£0.96	£1.01	--	£0.05	38.01%
08 February 2013	27 August 2013	PFC	£12.90	£13.51	--	£0.61	8.69%
	08 September 2013	CWC	--	--	£0.02	£0.02	
18 September 2013	20 September 2013	AGK	£15.79	£16.50	--	£0.71	823.84%
27 September 2013	28 March 2014	ULVR	£24.55	£25.54	--	£1.00	8.14%
02 December 2013	28 March 2014	ULVR	£24.33	£25.54	--	£1.22	15.72%
	12 November 2013	ULVR	--	--	£0.23	£0.23	
	12 November 2013	PVCS	--	--	£0.11	£0.11	
	03 December 2013	ULVR	--	--	£0.22	£0.22	
04 August 2014	14 August 2014	SBRY	£3.07	£3.25	--	£0.13	208.64%
04 November 2014	11 November 2014	VOD	£2.15	£2.16	--	£0.01	30.89%
06 May 2014	02 August 2019	CNA	£3.23	£1.35	--	-£1.87	-11.07%
22 May 2014	11 November 2014	VOD	£2.04	£2.16	--	£0.12	12.75%
	06 August 2014	VOD	--	--	£0.07	£0.07	
	11 December 2014	CNA	--	--	£0.05	£0.05	
24 November 2014	26 February 2015	PFC	£8.95	£9.16	--	£0.21	9.01%
13 March 2015	17 March 2015	PFC	£8.23	£8.56	--	£0.33	364.53%
	25 June 2015	CNA	--	--	£0.08	£0.03	
16 June 2015	23 June 2015	PFC	£8.84	£9.51	--	£0.67	393.51%
17 June 2015	06 August 2015	GSK	£13.50	£14.21	--	£0.71	38.22%
07 July 2015	16 July 2015	PFC	£8.67	£9.15	--	£0.43	226.26%
20 July 2015	28 August 2015	PFC	£8.64	£8.85	--	£0.21	22.65%
18 August 2015	10 September 2015	SSE	£15.25	£15.75	--	£0.50	52.39%
11 September 2015	20 October 2015	GSK	£12.90	£13.58	--	£0.63	49.17%
27 October 2015	04 December 2015	PFC	£8.50	£8.55	--	£0.05	5.96%

London Stock Exchange 2013 to 2017 (Continued)

Purchase Date	Sale / Dividend Date	Share	Buying Price / Share	Selling Price / Share	Dividend / Share	Gain / (Loss)	Return on Investment
06 November 2015	04 December 2015	PFC	£7.64	£8.55	--	£0.91	154.99%
	26 November 2015	CNA	--	--	£0.04	£0.04	
07 December 2015	16 December 2015	PFC	£7.59	£8.16	--	£0.57	303.71%
21 December 2015	23 December 2015	PFC	£7.49	£8.00	--	£0.51	1254.33%
06 January 2016	28 January 2016	PFC	£7.50	£7.75	--	£0.26	56.82%
09 February 2016	16 February 2016	PFC	£7.10	£7.61	--	£0.51	376.30%
11 March 2016	18 March 2016	MKS	£3.95	£4.16	--	£0.21	277.50%
16 March 2016	18 March 2016	WTB	£38.00	£39.50	--	£1.50	721.91%
06 April 2016	10 May 2016	EZJ	£14.73	£15.00	--	£0.27	19.64%
15 April 2016	20 April 2016	WTB	£36.95	£38.15	--	£1.20	237.08%
06 May 2016	05 August 2016	ISAT	£8.21	£8.51	--	£0.29	14.37%
13 May 2016	23 May 2016	EZJ	£14.40	£14.91	--	£0.51	129.33%
	27 May 2016	ISAT	--	--	£0.22	£0.22	
09 June 2016	30 June 2016	PFC	£7.47	£7.59	--	£0.12	27.97%
	23 June 2016	CNA	--	--	£0.08	£0.08	
04 July 2016	07 July 2016	WTB	£34.97	£35.81	--	£0.83	289.97%
05 July 2016	07 July 2016	PFC	£7.25	£7.65	--	£0.40	1007.16%
12 September 2016	03 November 2016	ISAT	£7.60	£8.00	--	£0.40	37.21%
22 September 2016	17 November 2016	NXT	£49.00	£51.77	--	£2.77	36.80%
	21 October 2016	ISAT	--	--	£0.16	£0.16	
08 November 2016	15 December 2016	WTB	£35.40	£36.51	--	£1.12	31.12%
21 November 2016	21 December 2016	ULVR	£30.98	£32.54	--	£1.56	61.09%
	24 November 2016	CNA	--	--	£0.04	£0.04	
	16 December 2016	WTB	--	--	£0.30	£0.30	
04 January 2017	04 January 2017	NXT	£41.74	£43.00	--	£1.26	1102.00%
04 January 2017	05 January 2017	MKS	£3.25	£3.31	--	£0.06	650.02%
04 January 2017	28 March 2017	NXT	£41.50	£43.00	--	£1.50	15.92%

London Stock Exchange 2013 to 2017 (Continued)

Purchase Date	Sale / Dividend Date	Share	Buying Price / Share	Selling Price / Share	Dividend / Share	Gain / (Loss)	Return on Investment
12 January 2017	03 September 2017	ISAT	£7.19	£7.50	--	£0.31	6.71%
07 April 2017	13 April 2017	NXT	£39.91	£41.81	--	£1.90	289.07%
20 April 2017	19 May 2017	SSE	£14.28	£15.06	--	£0.78	68.54%
12 May 2017	15 November 2019	PFC	£6.91	£4.06	--	-£2.85	-16.44%
22 May 2017	15 November 2019	PFC	£6.59	£4.06	--	-£2.54	-15.50%
	29 June 2017	CNA	--	--	£0.08	£0.08	
11 July 2017	01 August 2017	DNLM	£5.74	£6.15	--	£0.41	124.15%
10 August 2017	08 February 2019	BAB	£8.50	£5.23	--	-£3.26	-25.63%
	20 October 2017	PFC	--	--	£0.09	£0.09	
	30 November 2017	CNA	--	--	£0.04	£0.04	
11 December 2017	21 December 2017	ISAT	£4.44	£4.85	--	£0.41	339.88%
29 December 2017	03 January 2018	GOG	£14.84	£15.75	--	£0.91	446.13%

London Stock Exchange 2018 to Date

Purchase Date	Sale / Dividend Date	Share	Buying Price / Share	Selling Price / Share	Dividend / Share	Gain / (Loss)	Return on Investment
10 January 2018	21 November 2018	UU	£7.73	£7.85	--	£0.12	1.80%
	16 January 2018	BAB	--	--	£0.07	£0.07	
9 February 2018	11 June 2018	ISAT	£4.40	£5.31	--	£0.91	62.02%
	25 May 2018	PFC	--	--	£0.19	£0.19	
	25 May 2018	ISAT	--	--	£0.09	£0.09	
19 June 2018	26 June 2018	RPC	£6.75	£7.20	--	£0.45	349.96%
	28 July 2018	CNA	--	--	£0.08	£0.08	
10 July 2018	21 November 2018	UU	£7.40	£7.85	--	£0.45	16.64%
	3 August 2018	UU	--	--	£0.26	£0.26	
	10 August 2018	BAB	--	--	£0.23	£0.23	
	19 October 2018	PFC	--	--	£0.10	£0.10	
	22 November 2018	CNA	--	--	£0.04	£0.04	
3 December 2018	9 January 2019	SSE	£10.85	£11.21	--	£0.36	32.51%
	16 January 2019	BAB	--	--	£0.07	£0.07	
8 February 2019	3 June 2019	PFC	£4.00	£4.45	--	£0.45	35.91%
	24 May 2019	PFC	--	--	£0.19	£0.19	
	18 October 2019	PFC	--	--	£0.10	£0.10	
28 October 2019	3 January 2020	IMB	£18.06	£18.97	--	£0.91	27.31%
15 November 2019	3 January 2020	IMB	£17.30	£18.97	--	£1.67	71.70%
	31 December 2019	IMB	--	--	£0.72	£0.72	
17 February 2020		IMB	£18.00	Currently held	--		
13 March 2020		IMB	£16.64	Currently held	--		
13 March 2020	25 November 2020	RDSA	£12.43	£14.01	--	£1.58	18.05%
	31 March 2020	IMB	--	--	£0.72	£0.72	
22 May 2020	26 May 2020	IAG	£1.90	£2.34	--	£0.44	2100.96%
22 June 2020		RDSA	--	--	£0.11	£0.11	
30 June 2020		IMB	--	--	£0.21	£0.21	
01 July 2020	05 August 2020	BP.	£3.05	£3.13	--	£0.08	27.35%

London Stock Exchange 2018 to Date (Continued)

Purchase Date	Sale / Dividend Date	Share	Buying Price / Share	Selling Price / Share	Dividend / Share	Gain / (Loss)	Return on Investment
05 August 2020		IMB	£12.90	Currently held	--		
01 September 2020		IMB	£12.50	Currently held	--		
21 September 2020		RDSA	--	--	£0.12	£0.11	
30 September 2020		IMB	--	--	£0.21	£0.21	
28 October 2020		IMB	£12.35	Currently held	--		
15 December 2020		AZN	£74.98	Currently held	--		
16 December 2020		RDSA	--	--	£0.11	£0.11	
21 December 2020		AZN	£73.99	Currently held	--		
31 December 2020		IMB	--	--	£0.48	£0.48	
26 February 2021		IMB	£13.65	Currently held	--		
29 March 2021		AZN	--	--	£1.37	£1.37	
31 March 2021		IMB	--	--	£0.48	£0.48	
13 April 2021		GLO	£1.97	Currently held	--		

Made in the USA
Las Vegas, NV
07 November 2026

57673717R00079